WOODTURNING
FULL CIRCLE

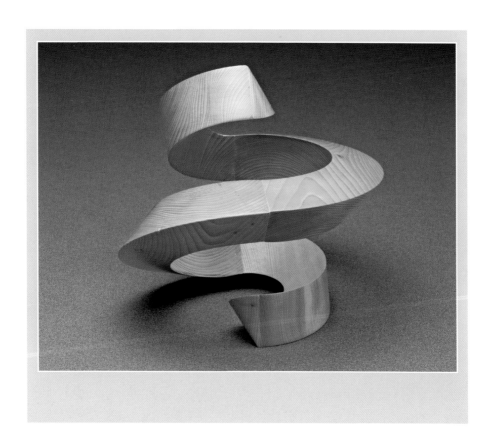

WOODTURNING
FULL CIRCLE

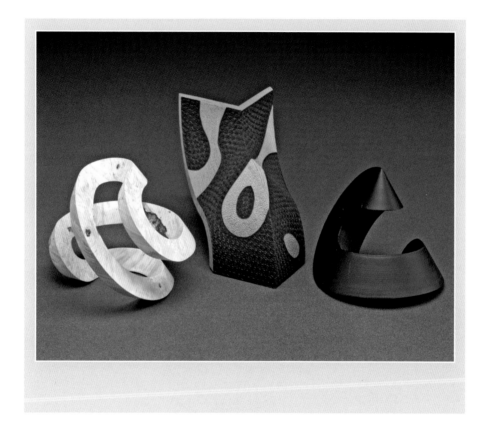

DAVID SPRINGETT

THE GUILD OF MASTER CRAFTSMAN PUBLICATIONS

This edition published 2008 by
Guild of Master Craftsman Publications Ltd
Castle Place, 166 High Street,
Lewes, East Sussex BN7 1XU

Reprinted 2014

ISBN 978-1-86108-531-3

Publisher: Jonathan Bailey
Production Manager: Jim Bulley
Managing Editor: Gerrie Purcell
Editor: Mark Bentley
Managing Art Editor: Gilda Pacitti
Designer: www.JoPatterson.com

Step-By-Step Photographs: David Springett
Studio Photographs: Gill Orsman
Illustrations: Robin Springett

Set in Stone

Colour origination by GMC Reprographics
Printed and bound in China.

Dedication
For Henk and Alice Rozenbroek, Vicki and Charlie Bradford. Great friends.

Measurements
Although care has been taken to ensure that the imperial measurements are true and accurate, they are only conversions
from metric. They have been rounded up or down to the nearest $1/32$in, or to the nearest convenient equivalent in cases
where the metric measurements themselves are only approximate and an appearance of greater precision
would be misleading.

When following the projects, use either the metric or the imperial measurements: do not mix units, because equivalents
are not exact. If you do work with imperial measurements it may be advisable to redraw the diagrams to provide
precise imperial measurements.

Health and Safety

- The projects described in this book are for enjoyment and pleasure. If simple commonsense rules are followed, that pleasure should be lasting.

- Always wear eye protection when turning wood or grinding metal.

- Don't forget the vital importance of protecting your lungs from the fine dust which is constantly produced when turning. Various masks are available; the better types filter the air and blow clean, cool air across your face behind a protective visor.

- Keep loose clothing and hair away from the lathe when working.

- If you use a three- or four-jaw metal chuck, be aware of those spinning jaws. Before the chuck is used on the lathe, remove the jaws and grind back the sharp external edges, then if the jaws hit the hand they are more likely to cause a bruise rather than a cut. In addition, paint the ends of the jaws white to make them more visible when the lathe is operating.

- Make absolutely certain that any screws used in wooden chucks are fully tightened before switching on the lathe.

- It is good practice to revolve the work by hand to ensure that nothing catches before switching the lathe on.

- Have the lathe and surrounding area well lit; if a deep cut is being made, use a light which can be moved easily to give the best illumination at all times.

- Do not over-extend the tool for deep cuts; try to reposition the toolrest for maximum support.

- Keep all tools sharp. Blunt tools are dangerous because they require more pressure.

- It is not safe to use a chainsaw without the protective clothing which is specially designed for this purpose, and attendance on a recognized training course is strongly recommended. Be aware that the regulations governing chainsaw use are revised from time to time; you must keep up to date.

- Do not use timber which may come apart on the lathe – beware of faults such as dead knots, splits, shakes, loose bark etc.

- Be aware that some woods can cause respiratory problems. Dust extractors and dust masks are most important, particularly when using spalted woods, which contain fungal spores.

- Some woods may cause skin irritation (iroko is a problem wood for me). If this happens, do not use that species again. Barrier creams, latex gloves and dust masks are advisable whenever you are using unfamiliar woods.

- Pay attention to electrical safety, and do not allow leads to trail where you, or others, might trip over them.

- Be particularly careful when disposing of any inflammable substances: wood shavings, finishing materials, oily rags, etc, are all potential fire hazards.

- Do not try to work when your concentration is impaired by drugs, alcohol or fatigue.

- Be sensible, take simple precautions, don't try to shortcut them. Enjoy your turning in safety.

Contents

Foreword

By Jean Francois Escoulen

Woodturning is unquestionably the fastest way of transforming material. You don't need much – with just a few tools in capable hands, the wood spinning in the lathe can take shape in a matter of hours, or minutes.

The woodturning lathe represents a most ingenious combination of speed and rotary movement. To turn an object, bearing in mind the characteristics of the wood and the original concept that defines the final form, requires patience, imagination and skill, as well as a sound understanding of how the tool works – for the tool is the vital intermediary between the hand and the machine.

Whatever level the turner is at, it is always possible to make confident progress in this art – the art of woodturning, practised for more than three thousand years! For this reason, woodturning is a real pleasure – a pleasure unrivalled by any other branch of woodwork. The woodturning lathe offers unlimited scope for creativity.

David Springett is our guide through this inexhaustible variety. An experienced turner, with a great gift for instructing others, he shows us with infinite patience how to create objects which are sometimes quite simple in appearance, sometimes complex, even unprecedented. His methodical approach demystifies these sometimes daunting projects. Clear explanations, accompanied by numerous drawings and photographs, help us to understand the ingenious construction of certain pieces.

The twisted 'streptohedron' forms excite the imagination. As well as reproducing the pieces described here, we can use them as a springboard towards new forms and ideas of our own, following the same principles.

This is how woodturning evolves, ignoring passing fads and easy effects. Such is the price of creativity. A pioneer among pioneers, David Springett shows us the best of this art, and he knows how to explain it and make it accessible to the rest of us.

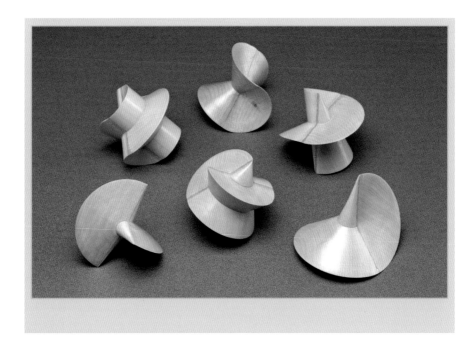

Introduction

I have been fortunate. When I felt that there was nothing new to be discovered in woodturning I came upon a sphericon. It was a small double cone which had been split along its axis, twisted (one half rotated through 180 degrees) and then rejoined. This shape was created by Colin Roberts in 1969.

The first time I saw this impossible object, I thought, 'This cannot be turned.' That was the wrong approach. I looked again and saw the possibilities. I looked at its basic cross-section and understood that other intriguing forms could be created, could be turned on the lathe, and that not all turned work is complete when the lathe is switched off.

I understand that not every woodturner will be as fascinated by these forms as I am, but that is not the point. Look at the turning processes described in this book, it is simple, plain turning. The piece is turned, it is split and rejoined – simple. Look at how these forms are created. Look at the much underused newspaper/glue joint which allows turned parts to be held in odd positions or to be split along their central axis or along other prepared lines. I explain how I turned these pieces, my method of working. If you have better ways of working, better methods for holding the work, use them. Please do not be discouraged by a perceived need for accuracy. This is wood that is being worked. It can shrink and swell. Certainly try for accuracy, but don't forget that mismatched joins can be carved to shape and that woodturning is supposed to be fun.

The aim of this book is not to provide completed projects which can be followed and reproduced (although it certainly does this), but to stimulate and encourage experiment and to create an understanding that lathe-turned objects can be something other than fully round. These shapes do not come to an end on the last page of this book; there are still numerous variations of these shapes that are waiting to be discovered. Daily I come upon new forms and new ideas.

I am grateful to a group of turners who have decorated some of my work and others who have either turned pieces to my design or have been working in a similar vein. They show the many possibilities of these shapes. I have tried to add practicality to the pieces: boxes, marble runs, puzzles and sculpture. It is up to you to see how you can develop these forms, how you can use your own favourite techniques to produce a unique piece of work. I hope that having seen some of the unusual shapes in this book you will realize that if you can think of it, it can be turned.

Part One: Background

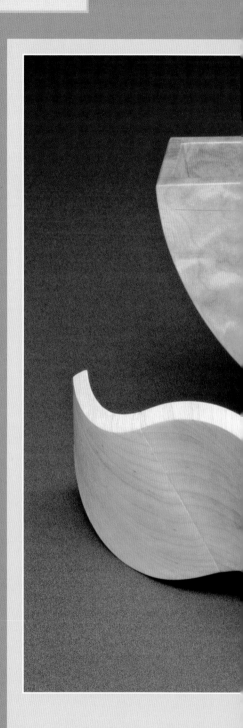

CHAPTER 1

WOOD

WOOD

As many of the pieces I turn rely on their form for impact I often choose plain woods and woods for their mechanical properties (for example castello boxwood which has very close grain and can be turned with thin, fine edges) rather than choosing woods which are highly figured or have showy grain. But, where possible, I try to choose woods which not only do the job I require but will also look good. Here is a list of the woods used in the projects.

African Blackwood *(Dalbergia melanoxylon)*

This dense, close-grained wood turns and finishes extremely well. It is a really lovely wood to work with and will take exceptional fine detail, but the dust – the fine black dust – will get everywhere. When you have finished polishing this wood ditch the polishing cloths, for they will carry the colour to other woods.

Ash and Olive Ash *(Fraxinus excelsior)*

I used to think that ash was just a common timber but recently, having used some excellent pieces, I have discovered that it works uncommonly well. It will take an excellent finish and has a most attractive grain. **BUT** olive ash is better still. The olive brown streaks running through the grain are magnificent, not overpoweringly showy but enough to grab attention.

Boxelder (Manitoba Maple) *(Acer negundo)*

I was given a piece of this wood by Simon Rossignol at a Quinte woodturners' guild (Ontario, Canada) meeting. The piece he gave me was a pale buttery yellow with a touch of burl and streaks of scarlet running through. I used this piece to good effect in a streptohedron Art Deco box. The wood turns and finishes well. If a Canadian friend asks what you want for Christmas, put this wood on the list.

Castello Boxwood *(Gossypiospermum praecox)*

Castello boxwood is sometimes mistakenly called lemonwood because of its creamy yellow colour. It is a wonderful wood to turn, taking fine detail. It is quite bland with little or no grain pattern. It has all the benefits of European boxwood and it is available in large, defect-free planks.

Maple. Tiger Maple. Quilted Maple (Acer)

Maple is a great turning timber. Its plain grain and creamy colour make it ideal for some of the work shown in this book. Tiger maple is a little more difficult to finish because the interlocking grain can tear out. Take care and the reward of the ripple or tiger effect is stunning.

Quilted maple can be spectacular. Sharp tools are essential as the grain travels in all directions and is easily torn. Problem areas where the grain is badly torn can be sanded out but this is not a method to be recommended. The piece, when all the turning is complete, can look quite flat *until* the finish is applied, then it becomes deep and three dimensional. It is best to use this wood where large, clear areas will show off that deep, rolling cloud effect.

Olivewood (Olea europaea)

I really like this wood even though it occasionally cracks and splits part-way through turning. It is quite greasy, like teak, but has wild black-brown streaky grain that is a wonder. Always clean the dust from your lathe immediately you have finished turning because I have read that the dust can be corrosive.

Padauk (Pterocarpus)

A great deep red colour when first turned with a light vanilla smell. Sadly, over time, it will begin to change to a dull brown and the scent also disappears quickly. This is a good wood which turns well, exhibiting a plain grain.

Pau Amarello (Euxylophora paraensis)

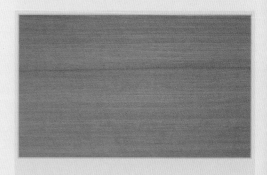

This was sold to me as yellow wood. It has very plain grain and its colour was closer to pale orange than yellow, but I was not disappointed for it is a quality wood. It is dense, easy to turn and easy to finish. I used it to turn the marble-run streptohedron where grain pattern would have been a distraction – the perfect choice.

Sonokeling *(Dalbergia latifolia)*

Indonesian rosewood. This wood has an attractive purple to brown colour. It turns and polishes extremely well. I have only used a small length of this wood and it compares well to true rosewood.

Tulipwood *(Liriodendron tulipifera)*

This is a real showy wood with bands of pink, red, brown and sometimes yellow running through in a swirling pattern. It is great to turn and easy to finish. As it is quite expensive I often use it for smaller pieces so that I will get value for money.

Walnut *(Juglans regia)*

This is a good-tempered wood which turns and finishes very well. It is dark brown in colour with good grain pattern. If you harvest your own timber, look out for crotches of walnut where the branches divide. The stress patterns created at the division of branches produce spectacular grain patterns.

Yew *(Taxus baccata)*

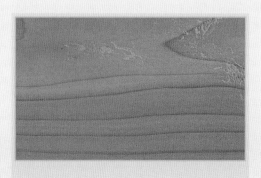

This well-patterned wood is a rich pinkish or reddish brown, sometimes with a pale red spreading sunset colouration in parts, though this, unfortunately, is rare. I turn some of this occasionally, for the joy of turning and for that wonderful smell which lingers in the workshop. Yew has a well-deserved reputation amongst turners.

CHAPTER 2

HOLDING
METHODS

The Newspaper and Glue Joint

1 The newspaper and glue joint is a much underused but extremely useful temporary holding method. The method is simple: two pieces of wood are joined together, flat face to flat face. The faces must be perfectly flat and true.

2 Glue is spread on each of the faces and a sheet of newspaper is placed between.

3 The two halves are then clamped firmly and the glue is allowed to dry overnight. (I prefer to use white carpenter's glue.) The joined block may then be turned as a normal, solid piece of wood. When the turning is complete the newspaper/glue joint is split using a knife. The sheet of newspaper, strong enough to hold together during turning, easily shears down its length, leaving two identical turned halves.

1

2

3

Simple precautions to take when split-turning

1 Draw pencil diagonals to locate the centre of the blank. This centre mark must fall on the newspaper/glue joint line. *Lightly* mark that centre point using a centre punch or awl. This will ensure that the drive dog and revolving cup centre will drop exactly onto the marked point.

Set the piece in the lathe between centres. At the headstock end make sure that the prongs of the drive dog are set either side of the joint line. Do not allow them to drop into the joint line or they could force that joint apart. At the tailstock end support the blank using a revolving cup centre.

2 As a precaution, bind the blank with cable ties for rough turning. These may be moved as the square blank is turned round.

1

2

3 Having turned the blank to the required diameter, remove the driving dog from the headstock and replace it with a chuck. Hold the blank in the chuck, supporting the work at the tailstock with a revolving cup centre. Using a chuck, in conjunction with a cup centre, to hold the newspaper/glued blank will make sure it is secure throughout the turning process. The blank may now be turned to the required shape. When finished it may be removed from the lathe and the newspaper/glue joint split.

3

Holding a Blank on a Wood Faceplate Using a Newspaper/Glue Joint

This method is most useful when a large diameter piece needs to be turned. Little wood is wasted as no allowance needs to be made for areas that may need to be gripped in a chuck. A reusable wood faceplate, held on a metal faceplate at the headstock, is turned flat and true. Accurately mark the centre of the prepared wood disc.

1

1 White carpenter's glue is spread on the surface of the wood faceplate and the prepared blank. The surface of the blank upon which the glue is spread must be planed flat.

2 A sheet of newspaper is placed between the two glued surfaces and the tailstock centre is brought forward to hold the blank on centre and to apply pressure whilst the glue dries. As soon as the glue has gripped and will not slip, place a large block of wood between centre and the blank so that the clamping pressure is more evenly spread. Leave the glue to dry overnight.

2

3 When the glue has dried the work may be turned with confidence. The finished piece (or part-finished as in this example) is removed using a knife which shears the newspaper/glue joint.

3

4 As a large area is gripped by the newspaper/glue joint, a knife does not always open that joint instantly. Thin softwood wedges tapped into the opening made by the knife will open the joint without marking the wood surface.

4

Workshop-Made Chucks

Here I will describe two simple, workshop-turned wood chucks which are used to hold awkward shapes (for example, a split half of a turned streptohedron). This will allow the flat faces of the streptohedron parts to be turned so that they can be made into box halves. Each chuck is used to hold parts which are the same shape. Different shapes will be used for each chuck described.

The first method shows how a streptohedron half may be firmly held in an epoxy car-body filler chuck. The second method describes how to make a polyurethane foam chuck. This also firmly holds the streptohedron half so that an accurate hollow may be turned into the 'split' face.

Car-Body Filler Chuck

One of the properties of these streptohedrons is that their extreme edges and points will touch and can be enclosed within a sphere. A streptohedron half will fit snugly into a hemispherical hollow.

Begin by measuring the diagonal on the split face of the streptohedron which will be held in the chuck. This measurement will provide the diameter of the hemispherical hollow into which the half will fit. For this example the measured diagonal will be 3in (76mm).

Cut a 4in (100mm) diameter disc of ¼in (6mm) thick MDF. This will be the collar to fit over and hold the streptohedron half in the wood chuck. Fix a 4¼in (105mm) diameter by 2in (50mm) thick block of wood to a metal faceplate and turn it to a clean 4in (100mm) diameter. Turn the face flat and true.

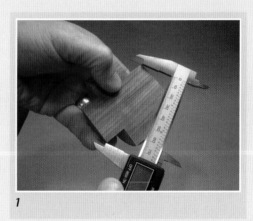

1

Into that face turn a 3in (76mm) diameter hemispherical hollow. Check that the streptohedron half will fit inside the hollow. Screw the ¼in (6mm) thick MDF collar centrally onto the face of the wood chuck. Mark a 2¾in (70mm) diameter pencil circle on the disc and turn, on the inside of that line, through to create a collar. Mark a datum line on the collar and the chuck so that they can be accurately realigned. On the face of the half-streptohedron mark pencil diagonals. This marked centre will help locate and hold the half exactly on centre. Picture 3 on page 21 shows a collar holding the streptohedron in place.

2

3 Cut a piece of plastic food wrap large enough to cover the split half. Mix the epoxy car-body filler (I used Bondo) and spread it into the hollow. Press the wrapped half into the hollow and fit the collar. Leave until the epoxy has set.

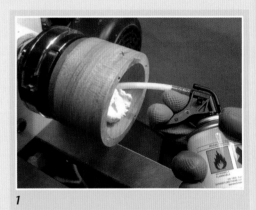
3

4 The last picture shows the half removed, leaving the epoxy shaping inside the chuck which will hold the half-streptohedron, and any other halves of the same shape.

4

Polyurethane Foam Chuck

Here is a simple chuck made from wood which uses the expanding, gap-filling insulation foam available from most hardware stores. A bespoke chuck made in the following way will hold all shapes and sizes. When the chuck is no longer needed the foam can be turned away and the hollow used again. The hemispherical hollow chuck and collar are produced as described above.

Mark pencil diagonals across the face of the split steptohedron half. Cover the streptohedron half in plastic food wrap with sufficient to extend beyond the edges of the chuck. This is necessary as the polyurethane foam which is to be used will glue parts together. The plastic film will prevent permanent fixture. The collar needs the plastic film protection as much as the split streptohedron half does.

1

1 Spray the polyurethane foam into the hemispherical chuck hollow. It is essential that rubber gloves are worn.

2 Press the plastic film-wrapped half into the foamed hollow, making sure that the plastic film covers the edges of the chuck.

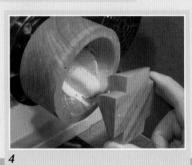
2

3

3 Screw the collar onto the chuck, trapping the split half. Make sure that the collar is evenly screwed in place so that the face of the split half is level with the top surface of the chuck. It is necessary to lock the split half in place for this compresses the foam as it dries giving a rigid hollow form into which the split half will fit. The revolving centre may be brought forward to check against the centre marked on the blank. Now is the time to make any adjustments. When the foam has dried (read the instructions on the can) the collar may be removed.

4

4 Remove the split half and turn the edge of the chuck to remove excess, hardened foam.

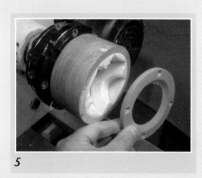

5

5 The last picture shows the now solid foam hollow and the collar waiting to be fitted. This chuck can be used to hold any half-streptohedrons of the same shape, or the foam can be turned away and the chuck reused.

Centre Bolt and Captive Nut

Using a central bolt to hold a blank allows the outer profile of a ring to be turned. Used in conjunction with shaped, angled, softwood blocks, the outer edge may be firmly held, allowing the inner profile to be turned. It is most important that the face of the blank, which seats against the wood faceplate, is flat and true so that the bolt, when tightened, pulls against the work evenly down. This is particularly important when using blanks with a newspaper/glue joint which is set across the centre line, for any uneven pressure could break that joint. The captive nut and bolt method of holding work requires that a nut is glued with epoxy resin, centrally, on the underside of a wood faceplate. The workpiece, with a central hole drilled through, can then be screwed onto the wood faceplate using a suitable sized bolt.

1 The workpiece may be temporarily joined to the wood faceplate with a newspaper/glue joint.

The benefits of a captive nut are firstly that the bolt may be removed from the front of the work, leaving the area around the central hole able to be turned; and secondly that only the bolt head shows above the surface of the work.

The disadvantages of the captive nut are that it is a time consuming process to fix the nut in place, and that fixing the nut to the back of the wood faceplate requires a pilot hole. The faceplate has to be removed once the pilot hole has been drilled. Next the underside is counterbored to accept the nut. The faceplate is then fixed back onto the metal faceplate, and onto the lathe, so that it can be drilled through to accept the bolt. The faceplate is removed once more so that the nut may be epoxy resin glued in place. When the glue has set, the faceplate is refixed to the metal faceplate and then to the lathe.

1

2 The carriage bolt method is simpler. A hole, which is the diameter of the coach bolt, is drilled centrally through the faceplate whilst on the lathe. A carriage bolt is pushed through from the back and tapped into place. The square section under the head of the carriage bolt is driven into the wood to prevent the bolt from twisting.

2

3 The workpiece, with a centrally drilled hole which matches the size of the bolt, is pushed onto the bolt and the nut is tightened.

The benefits of this method are that it is quick and simple. The disadvantage is that once the turning of the front face has been completed the bolt has to be knocked out through the hollow mandrel of the lathe, otherwise the bolt can interfere with parts turned close to the centre. Secondly, unless the bolt is cut to the exact length it will protrude from the work.

Whichever method is used, once the work is held on the bolt the edge and face may be safely turned.

3

Softwood Blocks and Hot-Melt Glue

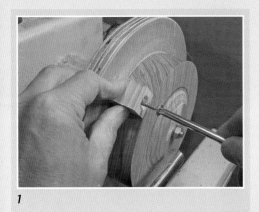

1. When an inner profile has to be turned, softwood blocks are fixed around the finished outer edge of the work.

2. If tacks of hot-melt glue are laid on the joint between the softwood blocks and the work, these will be sufficient to hold the work when the supporting bolt has been removed.

3. The central core can then be removed and the internal hollow may be turned to the required shape.

4. When the turning is complete the softwood blocks are unscrewed and lifted away. The polished surface of the turned ring provides the hot-melt glue with sufficient grip but does not allow it to penetrate beneath the surface making removal easy.

When rings with more awkward profiles are to be turned, the softwood blocks are cut with angled slopes matching those on the workpiece.

The piece may be reversed on the central bolt, allowing the second side to be turned. The softwood blocks will hold the outer ring, allowing the internal hollow to be turned once the supporting bolt (now redundant) has been removed.

CHAPTER 3

DRAWING SHAPES

DRAWING SHAPES

Triangle with Sides of Equal Length

There are alternative methods for drawing these shapes but I have tried to keep the process as simple as possible.

Method 1: Draw the base line to the required length. Using a 60° set square, mark a line from the right hand end of the base line sloping up to the left.

Again use a 60° set square and mark a line from the left hand end of the base line sloping up to the right. The two lines will cross at the apex of the equal sided (equilateral) triangle. If you do not have a set square then use the second method to draw an equal sided triangle with a pencil compass and rule.

Method 2: Draw the base line to the required length XY. Set the compass point on Y and open the compass so that the pencil touches the end of the line at point X. Draw a pencil arc above and over the centre of the line XY.

Set the compass point on X and open the compass so that the pencil touches the end of the line at point Y. Draw a pencil arc above and over the centre of the line XY. Where the two arcs cross mark as position Z. Join the positions X, Y and Z with a pencil line to produce an equal sided triangle.

Square

As an example a square with sides 2in (50mm) long will be drawn. Draw a line 2in (50mm) long. Mark one end A and the other B. Take a set square with a 90° angle and place it at point A so that a line may be drawn upwards from A at 90° to the line. Repeat at point B. Measure from A 2in (50mm) upwards on the vertical line and mark position D. Measure from B upwards on the vertical line and mark position C. Join C to D to complete the square.

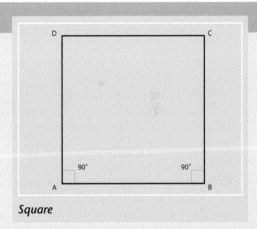

Square

Pentagon with Five Equal Sides

This shape baffles many of us, so follow this method. Draw a line AB the chosen length of side for the pentagon. Use a pencil compass to bisect (cut in half with a line at 90°) the line AB. Use a 45° set square and draw a line from B to cross the vertical bisector of line AB to obtain point C.

Use a 60° set square to draw a line from B to cross the bisector of line AB to obtain point D. Using a pencil compass, bisect the distance DC to obtain point E. Position E is the centre of a circle whose radius is EB. Draw that circle.

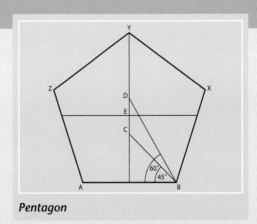

Pentagon

Set a pair of dividers to length AB (this is the chosen length of the side). Set the point on B and walk it around the circumference of the circle. This will provide five equally spaced points, ABXYZ, which when joined produce a regular pentagon.

Hexagon with Six Equal Sides

Draw a line of the chosen length of side. Mark one end A and the other B. Place the compass point on A and stretch it until the pencil tip touches B. With the point still at A, strike an arc upwards. Now, with the compass still set, place the compass point on B and strike an arc upwards. Where the two arcs cross will be the centre X. Place the compass point at X, as it is still set the pencil tip will touch both A and B. Draw a circle. With the compass still set, place the point on B and walk it around the circumference of the circle. This will provide six equally placed positions, A, B, C, D, E and F. Join those points to draw a regular hexagon.

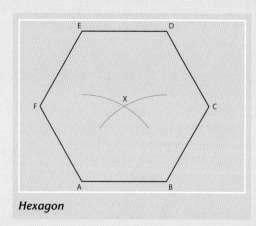

Hexagon

Three-Pointed Star

Draw an equal sided triangle as described above. Join positions X, Y and Z to the centre C.

Draw a small circle at the centre. The size of this circle will determine the base thickness of the star points. Where the circle crosses the line XC, mark it as x. Where the circle crosses line YC, mark it as y. Where the circle crosses line ZC, mark it as z.

Join X to y and z, join Y to x and z and Z to x and y. This will produce a three-pointed star. Increase or decrease the small circle to alter the shape of the star.

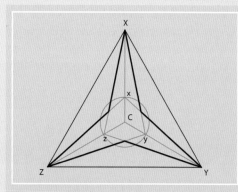

Three-pointed star

Four-Pointed Star

Draw a square as described above. Draw the diagonals.

At the centre C draw a small circle. The size of this will determine the base thickness of the star points. The letters Q, R, U and T indicate positions where this circle crosses the diagonals PW and OS.

Use a pencil and rule to join P to R and P to U. Join O to Q and O to T. Join W to R and W to U. Join S to T and S to Q. This will produce a four-pointed star. Increase or decrease the small circle to alter the shape of the star.

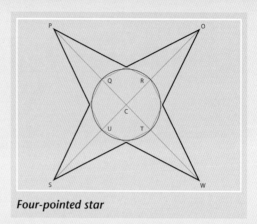

Four-pointed star

Five-Pointed Star

Draw the pentagon as described above.
Join point Y to A.
Join A to X.
Join X to Z.
Join Z to B.
Join B to Y.
This will produce a five-pointed star.

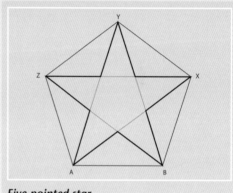

Five-pointed star

Six-Pointed Star

Draw the hexagon as described above.
Join point 1 to 3.
Join 3 to 5.
Join 5 to 1.
Join 6 to 2.
Join 2 to 4.
Join 4 to 6.
This will produce a six-pointed star.

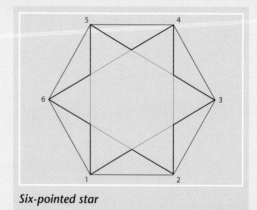

Six-pointed star

Legged Shapes

To produce the versions of these shapes which have wide, parallel sided leg forms, begin with the star shapes. Draw lines which radiate from the centre of the star to the tip of the points. Draw lines parallel to, and equidistant from, these radiating lines. Square them off at the tips.

Part Two: Projects

CHAPTER 4

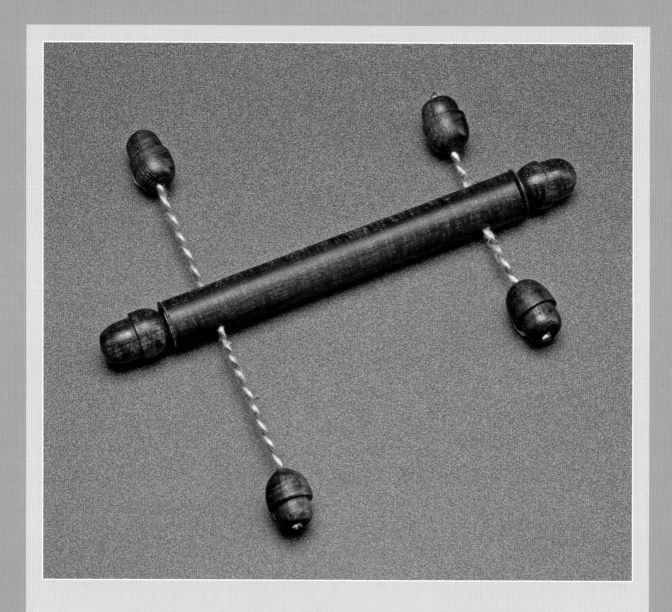

STRING AND STICK

This amusing little piece of turnery, which I first saw as an antique Chinese puzzle turned from bone, is quite simple to make from small pieces of wood. It's just a turned stick with different coloured strings threaded either end. Pull the blue string and it moves back and forth, as you would expect, but pull the red string and the blue string moves, stopping only when the acorn beads, attached at its ends, come up against the stick. Now pull the blue string and it can be pulled out of the stick pulling the red string until it too is drawn magically into the stick, and now the blue string can move back and forth freely. Is this magic or some devious trick? Find out, below, how this piece of fun is made.

It's the ideal project to use up some of those precious pieces of exotic woods that you have stored for years and just can't bear to throw away. Here I have used sonokeling (Asian rosewood) for just that reason.

What you will need

- Three pieces of exotic wood: two 4in (100mm) long by $7/8$in (22mm) square, and the other $4^3/4$in (120mm) long by $7/8$in (22mm) square.
- A piece of wood (for the supporting plugs) 4in (100mm) long by $7/8$in (22mm) square.
- Two 8in (200mm) lengths of different coloured thin string. You could buy white string and dye it different colours.
- 12in (300mm) of fine wire. Fine brass wire can be bought from a hobby store.
- Wood drills, $3/32$in (2mm), $11/64$in (4mm) and $1/4$in (6mm).
- A $1/8$in (3mm) round dental burr or similar fine drill.
- Candle wax.
- Typists' correction fluid.
- PVA glue and cyanoacrylate (super strong) glue.
- A small piece of card for marking templates.

Preparation

1. Take the 4in (100mm) length of wood, chosen for the supporting plugs, and holding it between a small chuck and revolving centre turn it to about 7/8in (22mm) diameter. Reverse the piece in the chuck so that the unturned square end may also be turned round.

2. Measure from the tailstock and mark with a pencil, first a position 7/8in (22mm) away and next, from that point, a position a further 1 3/16in (30mm) away. Turn this 1 3/16in (30mm) section down to 1/4in (6mm) diameter. Cut the 6mm diameter, 30mm (1 3/16in) wide section in half. Now set these two supporting plugs on one side.

Dimensions for end cap and stick

Turning the Stick

1. Take the 4in (100mm) length of 7/8in (22mm) square piece of exotic wood, hold it between chuck and revolving centre and turn it to about 7/8in (22mm) diameter. Using the nose point of a skew chisel, turn the tailstock end of the wood, square and true. Set a 1/4in (6mm) drill in a Jacobs chuck in the tailstock and drill, centrally, into the turned blank as deep as convenient but at least halfway.

   Reverse the piece in the lathe, centring the tailstock end carefully, and turn it to 7/8in (22mm) diameter. Square off the end and drill through, using the 1/4in (6mm) drill, until the holes meet up.

2. Fit the turned supporting plug into the chuck, making sure that it runs on centre. Fit the second supporting plug into the drilled hole in the turned stick, and bring up the tailstock for support.

3. Turn the stick down to 1/2in (12mm) diameter. Turn into the supporting plugs if necessary. Sand and polish the turned stick. Measure 13/32in (10mm) in from either end of the turned stick (from the junction of the stick and the supporting plugs), towards the middle of the stick, and make a light pencil mark. At both these positions, two 1/8in (3mm) holes, 180 degrees apart, are to be drilled.

1   I have used a 1/8in (3mm) round dental burr to drill the holes, for I find when drilling on a curved surface dental burrs are less likely to skid than ordinary drills. To arrange the holes so that they are at 180 degrees apart I rotate the chuck so that one jaw is top dead centre, then I drill on the marked position on the top of the stick. The chuck is then rotated so that the chosen chuck jaw is now directly at the bottom. The second hole may now be drilled on the top of the stick and the two holes will be 180 degrees apart. Repeat this procedure at the tailstock end. Remove the piece from the lathe and set aside.

4

Turning the Acorn Beads

1   Take the 4³/4in (120mm) long by 7/8in (22mm) square piece of exotic wood and hold in a small chuck, supporting the tailstock end with a revolving centre. Turn it to about 22mm (7/8in) diameter. Reverse the piece in the chuck, centre accurately, and turn the piece fully round.

Fit a 3/32in (2mm) drill into the Jacobs chuck and drill as deep as convenient (at least 25mm or 1 inch deep). Replace the small drill with a 5/32in (4mm) drill and, using typists' correction fluid, mark a point on this drill 5/32in (4mm) away from the tip.

1

2

Drill into the end of the turned wood until the white mark is reached. This forms a recess or counterbore to receive the knot on the end of the string. Withdraw the drill and bring the centre up to support the work. Turn at least 1³/8 in (35mm) of the wood down to an accurate 1/2in (12mm) diameter to match that of the stick.

2   On a piece of card accurately mark the acorn bead shape as shown in the illustration on page 32. Hold this template to the revolving wood and transfer the details using a pencil.

3

3   Slice into the wood to define the end part of the acorn, then turn the end part to 1/4in (6mm) diameter. Round over the acorn end.

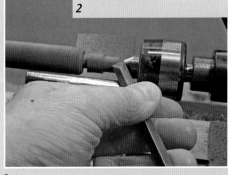

4   Round over the acorn top. Sand and polish, then part off.

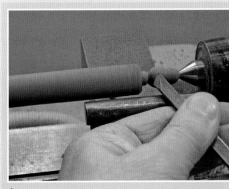

4

Turning the Acorn Finials

The picture right shows the acorn beads completed with the blank of wood (100mm or 4in long by 22mm or ⁷⁄₈in square) ready to turn the acorn finials.

1. Turn the blank fully round to a diameter of ⁷⁄₈in (22mm). Then turn the end down to an accurate ¹⁄₂in (12mm) diameter.

2. On a piece of card accurately mark the acorn finial as shown in the illustration on page 32. Use a pencil to transfer the important points to the revolving wood. Use a parting tool turn the ¹⁄₄in (6mm) diameter tenon which will fit into the drilled hole in the stick.

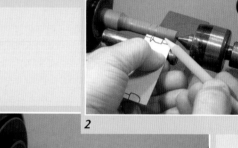

3. The end of the acorn is turned to ¹⁄₄in (6mm) diameter and rounded over at the tailstock end. Turn a fine collar between the ¹⁄₄in (6mm) tenon and the rounded end of the acorn.

4. Polish the acorn finial. Withdraw the revolving centre so that the end may be lightly turned to remove the centre mark, and then polish the turned end.

5. Part off, using a slim parting tool, on the headstock side of the turned tenon.

Threading the String

Cut two differently coloured 8in (200mm) lengths of thin string. Hold the string against the side of a candle and pull it along two or three times. This will lightly coat the string with wax and will act as a lubricant. Take a 12in (300mm) length of fine wire and fold it in half to create a loop at one end. Push this looped end through the 3/32in (2mm) hole end of an acorn bead.

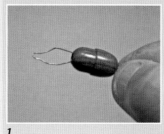

1

Thread the red string through the open wire loop. Pull the wire through the acorn bead, and the string with it.

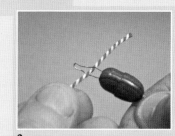

2

Continue to pull the string but, before it is pulled all the way through the acorn bead, tie a knot in its end (or perhaps a double knot so that it is large enough to prevent it being pulled right through the bead). Pull the knot into the 5/32in (4mm) hole in the outer end of the acorn bead.

3

Take the stick and hold it so the drilled holes at one end are ready to be threaded with the red string. Thread the loop end of the wire through both holes. Push the free end of the red string through the open wire loop.

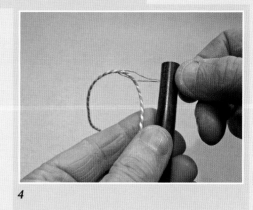

4

Pull the wire, and with it the string, all the way through the holes in the stick end.

5

6 Open the non-looped end of the wire and push one wire end down the hole in the stick so that it goes on one side of the red string, then push the other wire end back down the hole in the stick so that it is on the other side of the string.

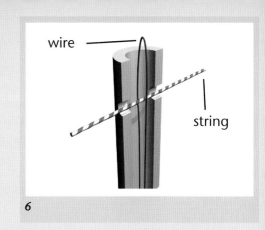

6

7 Push the wire down and pull it out of the end of the stick, bringing with it most of the red string, but not all of the red string. Some of the red string still remain threaded through both top holes.

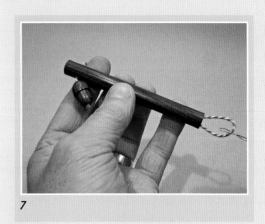

7

8 Pull the wire clear of the string. Now thread the loop end of the wire through the holes in the stick so that it goes through the loop formed by the red string. Thread the blue string into the wire loop.

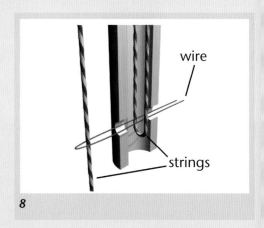

8

9 Pull the wire through the holes, and with it the blue string.

9

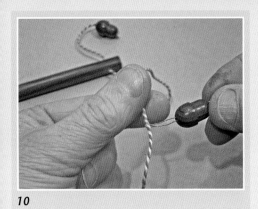

10

10 The remaining acorn beads are now threaded onto the red and blue strings in turn. Make sure that they are threaded on so that the 3/32in (4mm) larger hole faces out. Do not knot the ends yet.

11 Now pull the blue string so that the 'red' and 'blue' acorns (those with the knot inside) are pulled tight against the side of the stick.

11

12 Without pulling the string through, slide the 'red' acorn along the string so that it touches the stick. Pinch the string where it enters the acorn and hold that place.

13 Carefully, with that place still held, pull the string from the stick. Move the fingers from that 'pinched' place 3/8in (9mm) in towards the stick. At this new position tie a double (thick) knot and slide this knot into the 3/32in (4mm) hole in the end of the acorn bead end. Repeat this process at the blue string end.

12

Now pull the strings back and forth the check that the trick works. Now is the time to discover and rectify any problems. It can still be re-strung. When you are happy that all works well, the string ends showing at the acorn bead holes can be trimmed off and a small drop of super strong glue can be squeezed onto the knot, inside the bead, to secure it.

Finally, apply a little PVA glue to the tenon on the end of the acorn finial. Do not allow any glue to stray onto the end of the tenon, for this might make contact with the string when the tenon is pushed into place and cause problems. To complete, push the glued tenons into the ends of the tube. Clean off any excess glue. The piece is complete, so find an unsuspecting friend and baffle them.

13

CHAPTER 5

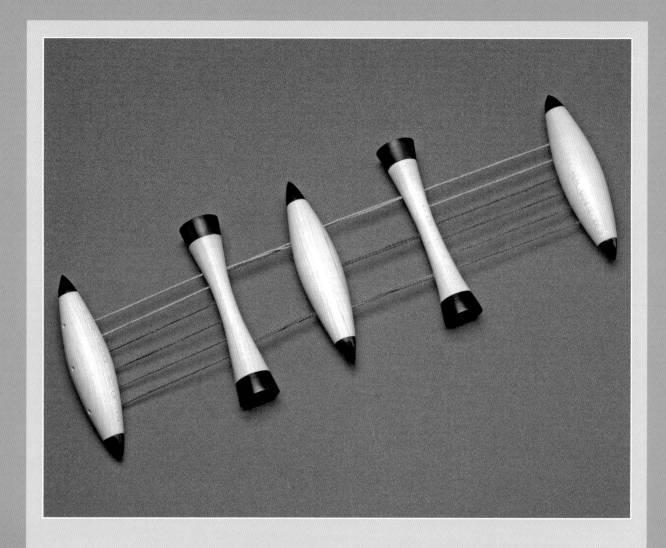

CHINESE STRINGS

I often visited the monthly antiques market at the Rag Market in Birmingham in the UK at a time when interesting pieces could be found at reasonable prices. I regularly saw small turned and carved sticks, usually made of bone but occasionally made from ivory, which had a series of small holes down both sides. The number of the holes varied on each side and on different sticks and when I asked what they were I was invariably told, 'They are Chinese counting sticks.'

During one visit I bought a small lacquered box which contained a selection of carved ivory puzzles and tricks and amongst those pieces were a number of bone Chinese sticks strung together. When the sticks (nine in all) were pulled downwards the numbers of strings (nine in all) would magically change, sometimes three strands, sometimes five, other times seven.

Looking closely, the illusion was apparent: the number of strands depended upon the holes in each stick and clever threading. When I showed my find to a magician friend he explained about these Chinese sticks. They had a story to go with them.

The story was to do with a monk in his cell. His windows were barred with nine bars (the nine strings) to prevent him from visiting the local village at night. He was becoming tired of being confined and so through his meditation was able to alter the number of bars to three. (Pull the next stick down to show three strings). This enabled him to leave for the night. On his return (pull the next stick to show nine strings) the nine bars were in place and so he had to meditate to reduce the number of bars to re-enter his cell.

The story continues in this manner until he is caught, locked out of his cell, having had such a drunken night that he is unable to meditate.

There are only five Chinese sticks in this project, with only six strings to thread. If you wish to be more adventurous then, having understood the reason for the number of holes and the method of stringing, any number of sticks with any number of holes can be made.

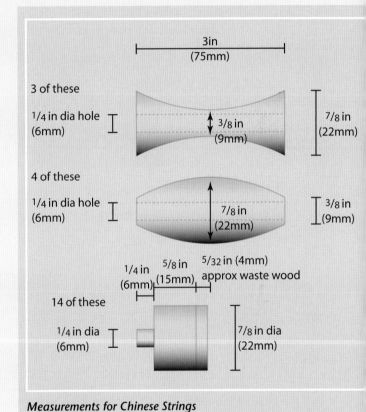

Measurements for Chinese Strings

2

What you will need

- **Five pieces of light coloured wood (I have used sycamore), 3in (75mm) long by 1in (25mm) square.**
- **Five pieces of dark wood (I have used African blackwood), 3in (75mm) long by 1in (25mm) square.**
- **A piece of wood (for the supporting plugs) 4in (100mm) long by 7/8in (22mm) square.**
- **Three pieces of different coloured string or thread, each 24in (600mm) long. I have used a Cotton Perle No 5. This may be bought from a shop selling embroidery threads.**
- **12in (300mm) of fine wire. Fine brass wire can be bought from a hobby store.**
- **A small crochet hook.**
- **A 1/8in (3mm) round dental burr or similar fine drill.**
- **Candle wax.**
- **Typists' correction fluid.**
- **PVA glue and cyanoacrylate (super strong) glue.**

Preparation

Take the 4in (100mm) length of wood chosen for the supporting plugs, and turn them as shown in Chapter 4 under Preparation.

Turning the Fat Cigar Shaped Sticks

1. Take a 3in (75mm) by 1in (25mm) square piece of sycamore and hold in a small chuck. Support the tailstock end with a revolving centre. Turn the piece round to about 1in (25mm) diameter, then reverse in the chuck to complete the rounding up. Use a skew chisel to square off the end.

1

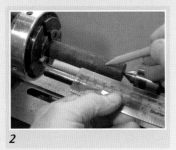

2

3

4

5

6

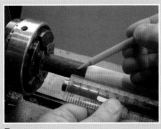

7

Fit a 1/4in (6mm) twist drill in the Jacobs chuck, held in the tailstock, and drill centrally at least 2in (50mm) into the rounded sycamore. Reverse the piece in the chuck and re-centre. Using the 1/4in (6mm) drill, still held in the Jacobs chuck, drill into the body of the wood until the holes meet. Work the remaining four pieces of sycamore in the same manner.

Now take a piece of the blackwood and hold it between the chuck and revolving centre. Round it down to about 1in (25mm) diameter. Reverse it in the chuck so that the unturned end may be rounded.

2 Measure from the tailstock end towards the headstock, 13/16in (20mm) followed by a further 13/16in (20mm), marking in pencil at both these positions.

3 The second 13/16in (20mm) area may be turned down to 1/4in (6mm) diameter with a parting tool.

4 Carefully saw through the midpoint of the 1/4in (6mm) area, making sure that the part held in the chuck remains on centre.

5 Take one of the sycamore pieces and push it onto the 1/4in (6mm) turned blackwood dowel at the headstock end. Fit the other blackwood piece into the 1/4in (6mm) hole in the sycamore, bringing the revolving centre up to support the work.

6 Carefully turn the whole piece round, bringing it to 7/8in (22mm) diameter. Measure halfway along the sycamore piece and mark a light pencil line.

7 At the headstock end, mark a position 3/8in (9mm) on the headstock side of the junction between light and dark wood. Using a fine parting tool turn down, on the headstock side of that line, to about 3/8in (9mm) diameter. At the tailstock end, mark a position 3/8in (10mm) on the tailstock side of the junction between light and dark wood. Use a parting tool turn down, on the tailstock side of that line, to about 3/8in (9mm) diameter. These two parting cuts delineate the length of the stick.

8 From the marked centre line on the sycamore piece turn, with a fluent convex curve, towards the headstock, aiming to finish at the section that has been turned down. It is not necessary to turn all the way, just aim for that point. Continue turning the convex curve, regularly checking the diameter at the junction of the light and dark wood. When that diameter is 3/8in (9mm) the curve should be correct.

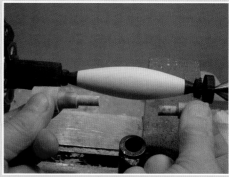

8

9 Now turn from the centre of the sycamore piece towards the tailstock, repeating and reflecting that fluent convex curve to produce a fat cigar shape. Sand and polish the work. If you are concerned about dragging dark polish into the light sycamore then the sycamore piece may be removed from between the blackwood pieces and held between the light wood supporting plugs (made earlier) when polishing.

9

10 When removing and separating (temporarily) the dark and light wood pieces, it is a good idea to mark the ends of the dark wood dowels with typists' correction fluid. Make a mark on that surface and a corresponding mark on the light wood so that, should they become separated, they can easily be reunited. Using a fine blade parting tool, part off the blackwood turned end which is held in the chuck. Leave sufficient to allow the point to be fully turned later.

10

11 At the headstock, replace the chuck with a Jacobs drill chuck. Hold the blackwood part-turned ends in the Jacobs chuck, gripping the 1/4in (6mm) turned end. Turn the blackwood piece to a point which should end at the position marked by the original parting-off line. Sand and polish.

11

12 The pointed ends may be pushed into place, to complete the fat cigar shape, but be careful – do not push them fully home because if they are a good fit they may not be easily pulled out. If you are faced with the problem of having a pointed end stuck fast then wear some rubber gloves, they will give the extra grip necessary to help pull the end away from the body. Now turn the other two fat cigar shaped pieces in a similar manner.

12

Turning the Two Matching Concave Sticks

The two sycamore pieces have been prepared so:

1 Take a blackwood piece and hold it between chuck and revolving centre. Round it down to 1in (25mm) diameter. Reverse it in the chuck and turn a ¹³/₁₆in (20mm) wide section, ¹³/₁₆in (20mm) away from the tailstock end, down to ¹/₄in (6mm) diameter as previously described. Cut through this turned section so that two parts are produced, each with a ¹/₄in (6mm) tenon.

1

Fit the sycamore piece between these blackwood pieces and turn to ⁷/₈in (22mm) diameter. Mark a pencil line ³/₈in (10mm) from the light/dark wood junction on the dark side of that junction. Using a parting tool, turn down to about ³/₈in (9mm) each time, on the side away from the sycamore junction. This position delineates the length of the finished stick.

Use a pencil to lightly mark the centre of the sycamore piece. Turn from either blackwood end towards the centre mark to produce a gentle concave curve which will match that of the fat cigar shape. Understand that you do not have to be too precise in matching the convex and concave curves of these shapes. Even if the curves don't precisely match, your eye will suggest to your brain that they look as though they do. The thinnest part of the central sycamore section should be about ³/₈in (9mm) diameter.

2

Carefully sand and polish. If you wish to avoid dragging any colour from the blackwood, use the supporting plugs to hold the sycamore when polishing. The blackwood ends are fully parted off, using a thin parting tool, at the previously marked positions (9mm or ³/₈in away from the junction of the light and dark woods).

2 Apply a dab of typists' correction fluid to the end of the blackwood tenon, marking it and the matching sycamore end with a corresponding figure so that if they should become separated they can be reunited.

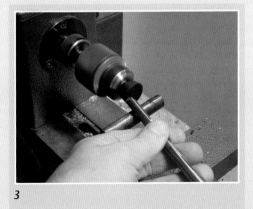

3

3 Remove the chuck from the headstock and replace it with a Jacobs chuck. Hold the parted-off blackwood piece on the turned tenon and turn its face flat and true. Fit the now completed blackwood ends onto the sycamore centre. Now turn the second concave stick.

Marking and Drilling the Sticks

Here I will explain a general method of setting out the hole positions and drilling those holes. This method can be used on each stick once you have marked out the correct number of hole positions. For the measurements used to set out the holes, see the illustration. Be consistent with the method of marking out the holes so that they will line up easily. The sticks are arranged as follows:

Cigar-shaped with six holes on one side.
Concave with six holes on one side and three on the other.
Cigar-shaped with three holes on one side and two on the other.
Concave with two holes on one side and six on the other.
Cigar-shaped with six holes on one side and three on the other.

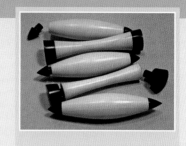

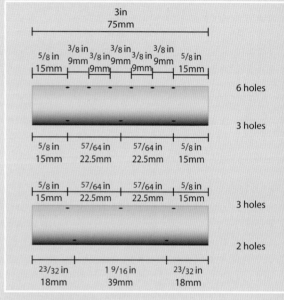

Sizes to set holes

1 The first stick is held in the lathe between the supporting plugs. The grain is aligned in the same direction each time a new stick is placed between the plugs. This will ensure that all the sticks have similar grain markings facing front. The top dead centre is marked on the supporting plug so that the line of holes at the top can be marked. Directly opposite (beneath, 180° away) bottom dead centre is marked on the supporting plug so that the second line of holes (if needed) can be marked. Here the six positions can be seen marked out on a cigar-shaped stick and a bradawl is used to mark each point clearly.

2 A ⅛in (3mm) round dental burr, held in a flexible drive, is used to drill the holes vertically at each point. The concave shaped sticks are treated in exactly the same way. When all the sticks have been drilled then the threading can begin.

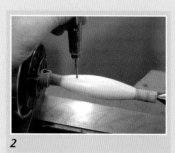

Threading the Sticks

Take three 24in (600mm) lengths of thin string or thread, each a different colour. Pull each length through a piece of candle wax to help it run smoothly through the holes.
A 12in (300mm) length of fine wire is folded to make a loop in one end and a small crochet hook is made ready to help pull threads through holes.

Top tips

- Always work the holes nearest the centre of the stick first, then work outwards.

- Keep the threads in line as they progress through the sticks; they must not cross over one another. For example, if a thread has begun in hole five it must continue through any hole five in the future. If it starts on the right then keep it on the right; this will prevent tangles.

- It helps to pull the thread out of the end of the stick after it has been threaded through the incoming hole. It can then be more easily directed (by wire loop or crochet hook) into the next, outflowing hole.

- The crochet hook can sometimes split the thread, so use it carefully. Try to use the wire loop in preference.

- Unfortunately it is only after having successfully threaded the first set of five sticks that an efficient strategy is worked out, so be patient.

- Do not be put off if the threading method is initially awkward. It will become much easier as you progress.

Now for the Threading

This is not a complete threading guide; it shows the principles which are to be applied to the sticks, the threads and the various holes as they are approached.

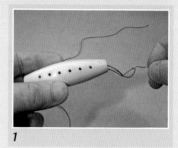

1

1 Begin with the cigar-shaped stick with only six holes. It has only one set of holes so that the ends of the thread loops can be neatly concealed inside. Using the wire loop, pull the green thread all the way through the drilled centre of the stick.

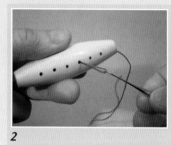

2

2 Pull the green thread through hole number three using a crochet hook so that one end hangs free. The picture shows the thread beginning to be pulled through.

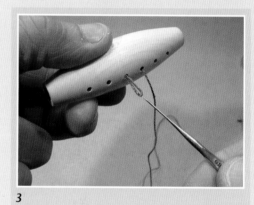

3

3 Next, using the crochet hook, pull the green thread through hole number four.

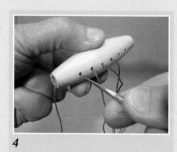

4

4 Now pull the red thread through hole number five, then through hole number six. Thread blue thread through holes one and two.

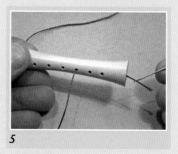

5

5 Now move on to the concave stick with six and three holes. Begin on the six hole side. Pull the green thread (from cigar hole number three) into concave hole number three and out of the end.

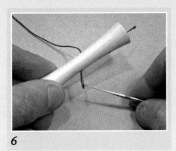

6 Next pull that same thread through the centre hole on the three-hole side. Pull the green thread from cigar hole number four) into concave hole number four and out of the end. Pull that same thread through the centre hole opposite to join its companion green thread.

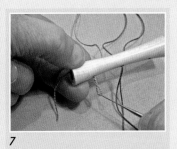

7 Now take blue thread number two and thread it into hole number two and out of the end of the stick. Using a crochet hook, carefully pull that same thread through hole number one on the opposite side of the stick. Next, pull the blue thread number one into hole number one to join the companion blue thread out the other side. Next, pull the red threads through the holes on the opposite end of the stick in the same manner.

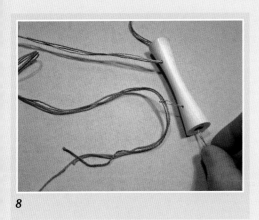

8 When a bundle of three threads needs to be pulled through a hole, treat them as a single thread. Using the wire loop makes the process easier. The bundle of threads can be pulled out through the end of the stick and then threaded individually if necessary.

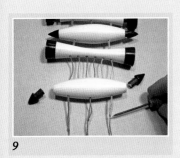

9 On the final cigar, stick the pairs of red, green and blue exit the holes. A knot is tied in each pair at the same distance from the stick. When satisfied that this is correct, touch each knot with a drop of super strong glue to seal it.

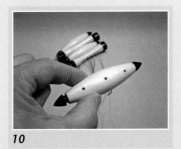

10 Trim off the loose ends and pull the knots into the holes to conceal them inside the stick. Test the Chinese sticks and, only when completely satisfied that all runs smoothly, apply a small drop of PVA glue to each blackwood tenon and push home to seal the stick ends.

CHAPTER 6

CHESS SET

CHESS SET

Like most turners I have wanted to make a chess set but have been discouraged, partly because I could never find a good looking set I really wanted to turn. However, the main reason for not attempting a set was that making the knight always posed a problem. Are the knight shapes cut on a fretsaw? Then do they all match? Are they fully carved from a single block? Is a compromise reached where they are turned to some representational shape and so not look horse-like?

In the latter case, every time the set is used a lengthy explanation has to follow that the odd-looking piece is really a knight. Well here is the answer. A traditional method of turning is used in a new way: ring or hoop turning, a technique developed and practised in the Erzegebirge mountains in eastern Germany for mass-producing wooden toys and animals. A profiled ring is turned, much like a circular picture frame, so that each time a slice is taken across the ring an exact copy of that first slice is produced.

By adapting this method, those awkward knights can be turned. By splicing two different coloured woods together to form a block before turning, matching knights for both sides of the chessboard can be produced in one go.

Traditionally the rings or hoops were turned with the grain running vertically. This allowed the pieces to be separated by splitting. Nowadays, the grain can run horizontally as the pieces can be bandsawn apart. This means that the work will be similar to turning the inside and outside of a bowl.

The chess set design is taken from a set which was recovered from the wreck of the ship *James Matthews*, which sank in Cockburn Sound, south of Fremantle on the west coast of Australia, in 1841.

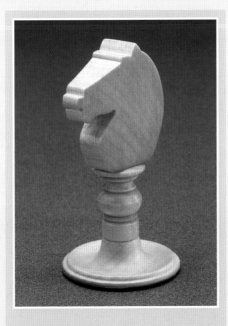

What you will need

■ A 4in (100mm) long by 3/8in (9mm) diameter Allen bolt, washer and matching nut. This bolt may be shorter, in which case counterbore to set the head below the surface.

■ A 1/8in (3mm) wide square-end tool which can be ground from a cheap imported wood chisel.

■ A 1/2in (12mm) cheap wood chisel ready to grind to shape. This will be needed to reach the awkward turned areas under the knight's chin.

■ For the wood faceplate, choose a piece of 8in (200mm) square by 3/4in (18mm) thick plywood.

■ Two 2in (50mm) long, countersunk No 8 screws.

■ A 2in (50mm) plug cutter (optional).

■ Epoxy resin glue.

■ A junior hacksaw and a triangular file.

■ Two blanks of different coloured hardwood, each 7³/₁₆in (180mm) long by 3⁹/₁₆in (90mm) wide by 1⁹/₁₆in (40mm) thick. I have chosen to use walnut and maple.

Preparation

Cut eight walnut and eight maple pieces, 2³/₈in (60mm) long by 1/2in (12mm) square for the pawns.
For the castles, cut two walnut and two maple pieces 3³/₁₆in (80mm) long by 25mm (1in) square.
The stems of the knight are turned from pieces 2in (50mm) long by 1in (25mm) square, so cut two each of these in both walnut and maple.

For the bishops, cut two walnut and two maple pieces 2³/₄in (70mm) long by 3/4in (20mm) square.
The queens are turned from one walnut and one maple piece, each 3⁹/₁₆in (90mm) long by 1in (25mm) square.

Cut two pieces 3⁹/₁₆in (90mm) long by 1in (25mm) square for the kings, one of each in walnut and maple.
Although I used walnut and maple, any two good-quality hardwoods, dark and light, could be used.

Making the Wooden Faceplate

1 Cut a 200mm (8in) diameter disc from the ³⁄₄in (18mm) thick plywood.

2 Mount this disc centrally on a metal faceplate, turn the edge clean and drill a pilot hole through its centre.

3 Mark a datum on the wood disc and the metal faceplate and remove the plywood disc. Counterbore the pilot hole on the back of the plywood disc to accept the nut for the Allen bolt.

4 Re-fit the plywood disc, aligning the datum marks, and drill through using a ³⁄₈in (9mm) drill.

5 Remove the plywood so that the nut may be glued in place using epoxy resin glue. When the glue has dried re-fit the plywood (remember the datum marks) to the metal faceplate.

The Knight

Preparing the blank

1 Make sure that one edge of each of the 7³⁄₁₆in (180mm) long walnut and maple blanks is planed flat and true, then glue those edges together. This will make a 7³⁄₁₆in (180mm) square by 1⁹⁄₁₆in (40mm) thick piece.

When the glue has set, measure along the joint line, find the centre, set a pencil compass to 3⁹⁄₁₆in (90mm) radius, then draw a pencil circle about that centre. Take the wood to the bandsaw and cut out the circular blank. At the marked centre drill a ³⁄₈in (9mm) hole. I have counterbored the hole first so that the head of the bolt is set below the surface, although this is not absolutely necessary.

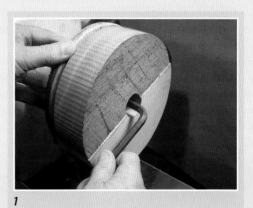

1

Bolt the blank firmly to the plywood faceplate. This single bolt will be sufficient to hold the work whilst the edge is turned. If you are uncertain about the holding ability of a single bolt, then screws may be fitted either side of the bolt. Turn the edge of the blank fully round.

2 Mark a pencil line 1³⁄₈in (35mm) from the junction of the plywood disc and the blank. Turn the face of the blank down to this line. Check that the turned face is flat and true, and that the blank is 1³⁄₈in (35mm) thick.

2

Marking Out and Shaping the Blank

The shape of the knight's head will be produced by establishing key points on the profile. These points will be connected to create the desired shape, dot–to–dot turnery. In two instances one key point will fall vertically beneath another. To help you locate both points accurately I will refer to the 'ear side' (in the direction of the ear) or the 'centre side' (towards the centre of the blank) of that vertical line. (Note that the head will face in towards the centre of the blank.) Pencil circles are used as a guide to the position of these key points. For example, position C will be located ³⁄₈in (9mm) directly below the pencil circle, line C, on the face of the work.

The knight will stand upright 'inside' the blank, so the top of its head will be facing towards the tailstock. All radius (or diameter) lines will be measured from the outer edge of the blank. All depth measurements are taken from the top surface of the blank.

As it is sometimes difficult to judge the shape of the knight whilst it is being turned, it may be helpful to cut out a series of part profile templates from card. These can be set against the shape as it is turned to check accuracy.

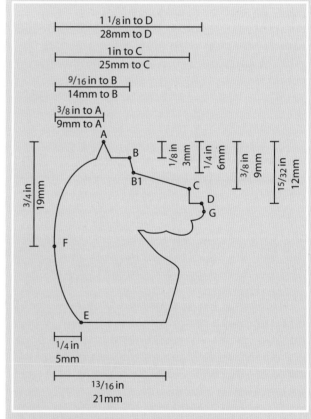

Outer profile dimensions for ring-turned knight

Turning the Top of the Profile

1 To locate the top point of the ears mark a pencil line, line A, 3/8in (9mm) from the edge of the blank.

Line B, the end of the forehead, is set 9/16in (14mm) from the edge of the blank. Line C, the end of the nose, is set 1in (25mm) from the edge of the blank. Line D, the end of the lip, is set 13/32in (28mm) from the edge of the blank. The picture shows these pencil circles being set out.

1

2

2 On the ear side of line B, using the 1/8in (3mm) wide square end tool, cut a groove 1/8in (3mm) deep. Here you will notice that a shelf toolrest is used to support the square end tool. This form of toolrest prevents the tool from being dragged down into the work.

3 On the centre side of line C, using the square end tool, cut a 1/8in (3mm) groove 3/8in (9mm) deep. On either side of line A measure 1/16in (1½mm). Turn a 1/8in (3mm) deep groove at these marked points, in each case on the side away from the ear. On the centre side of the ear, this cut will join with the cut previously made at line B. Make sure this new flat area is cleanly cut.

3

4 From line A turn a slope, from the pencil line, down on either side to meet the start of the cuts that have just been made. These slopes will produce the pointed ear.

4

5 On the side of the blank, at the junction of the blank and the plywood disc, turn a $3/16$in (5mm) deep, $1/8$in (3mm) wide groove. This locates position E at the base of the back of the knight. The picture shows the groove position. On the side of the blank measure, from the top face down, $3/4$in (19mm) and mark a pencil line, line F. This marks the centre of the back of the knight.

5

6 Now turn from the base of the ear up to line F in a good, clean, fluent curve.

6

7 To complete the curved back of the knight, turn from position E, at the junction of the blank and the plywood disc, up to line F. Cut a good, fluent curve.

7

8 To position the top point of the nose and to form the brow, turn a $1/4$in (6mm) deep, $1/8$in (3mm) wide groove on the centre side of line B. Join this new position to point C with a clean sloping cut. This will form the top of the nose.

Cut down to position G, which is a deep cut past the front of the lips on the centre side of line D. It is $5/8$in (15mm) deep and $3/8$in (9mm) wide, towards the centre. This wider cut is made to accept the parting cut from the other side once the blank has been flipped over.

Clean up the part-turned profile. To ensure that the blank will sit flat when removed and reversed on the faceplate, turn away a little of the central area. If the area around the bolt has not been counterbored then turn as close as possible to the bolt head and when the bolt is removed any unturned wood from beneath the bolt head may be chiselled away.

8

9 When satisfied that the profile and the surface finish are both good, undo the Allen bolt and remove the part-turned blank.

9

Turning the Underside of the Profile

To help fix the reversed, part-profiled ring to the plywood disc, drill and countersink two holes to accept the 50mm (2in) No 8 screws in the turned piece. The screws should go through the centre of the base section of the knight, straight down through the ears and into the plywood disc. They should be fully countersunk, if not slightly counterbored, so that no metal of the screw is showing. These screws are fixed on a line that will not be turned and will therefore be safe. If one screw is set on the walnut side of the joint line and one on the maple side, the blank will remain fully secure even when the ring is parted through and the centre portion removed. You may, if you wish, set a screw on each side of the joint line (four in all) for added security. The central bolt will hold the blank in place for the majority of the turning process.

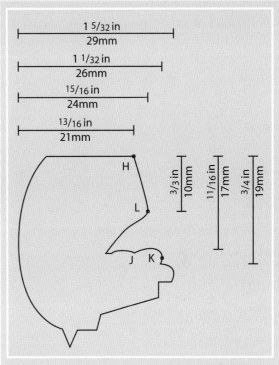

Dimensions for inner profile of ring-turned knight

1 Measure the diameter of the ears, line A, and make a note of this. Mark the ear diameter on the face of the plywood faceplate. Using the corner of the square end tool cut a vee groove on that marked diameter, so that (a) the tips of the ears are gently supported, but more importantly, (b) that the reversed blank is located accurately and centrally.

Fit the reversed blank onto the plywood disc, locating the ears in the prepared groove. Fix the central bolt in place and, when satisfied that the work is running on centre, screw the blank down.

Now the inner profile of the knight may be turned. For the dimensions, see the illustration.

Now the blank is fixed, measure 13/16in (21mm) from the extreme outer edge towards the centre and mark a pencil line. This is line H. Next measure and mark a pencil line at 15/16in (24mm) from the outer edge of the blank. This is line L. Measure and mark, from the same outer edge, a further pencil line at 1in (26mm) for line K. At line L turn a 1/8in (3mm) groove 3/8in (10mm) deep to locate the front of the knight's chest.

1

2 Now join point H (on the pencil line marked 24mm or ¹⁵/₁₆in in from the edge) to point L with a straight, clean cut. The next ¹/₄in (3mm) groove is cut on the centre side of line K to locate the lips. This groove is turned ³/₄in (20mm) deep. Remember to keep the tool sharp and to widen the groove when cutting deep. Now part through at 1¹/₂in (38mm) in from the edge. Cut on the centre side of this line. A small amount of waste wood will remain on the edge of the lip of the knight.

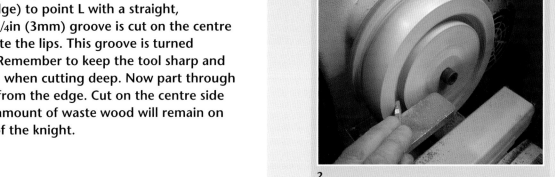

2

3 Remove the central core.

3

4 Turn away the waste wood above the chin area. Removing this waste wood will allow the area below the chin to be shaped. Turn the underside of the lip, opening the mouth slightly. Then turn the underside of the jaw.

4

5 To reach into that area where the front of the chest meets the jaw, grind a suitable shape on a cheap ¹/₂in (12mm) wood chisel. Relieve the edges of this tool so that it cuts efficiently. Take care when using this shaped tool. Slice from the top and the underside so that the tool cuts rather than scrapes. The final cutting, right into the corner between the jaw and chest, may have to be finished with a scraping action.

5

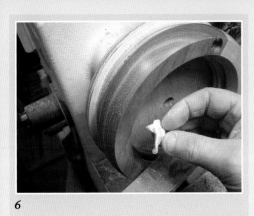

6

6 Check the profile under the chin and chest by pushing moulding material into the gap. Push the moulding material into the hollow, withdraw carefully so that the moulded shape is not distorted, check the profile and adjust if necessary.

7

7 Sand to a clean finish and, when fully satisfied, remove the ring. Still the profile cannot be seen! Remember, it is not essential to stick rigidly to the dimensions given. If a better shape can be seen or achieved when turning, that's fine, but be sure it is a better shape as it is too late when it is being sliced later.

What is interesting about this turning is the degree of accuracy required to produce this apparently meaningless series of ridges, grooves, coves and beads in order to create the shape within – a shape that cannot be seen until that exciting moment when it is too late to change, and the finished ring removed from the lathe lies on the bandsaw waiting to be cut.

So this is it. The smooth-ridged ring is ready for slicing. Each cut must be made towards the imagined centre of the ring. The nose faces the centre so that the knight's body will taper from its thicker, heavier back to the smaller, more pointed nose.

Cutting the ring segments

1 Cut first through the main part of the walnut at a point 90° from the joint, all the way across the imagined centre and across through the maple. The two halves open up to reveal the shape – success or failure in that one cut.

2 The next cut is made on the walnut side, 1/2in (12mm) away from the first, again towards the imagined centre, followed by another cut the same distance away.

3 Repeat for the maple, and four knight profiles lie on the bandsaw table waiting to be cleaned up.

4 Take a sheet of medium sandpaper and lay it upon a flat surface. Take one of the knights and lay it upon the sandpaper, cut side down. Rub until the surface is smooth, then repeat for the other side and the other pieces. The knight may either be carved or left as a simple profile.

1

Turning the Remaining Chess Pieces

I like to reduce my reliance on large pieces of equipment such as heavy metal chucks where I can. For me these tend to impede the free movement of the tool and hand whilst turning. So in many cases I use the larger chuck to hold pieces so that they may be roughed down to size or so that a holding spigot may be turned on one end. The piece may then be transferred to a smaller chuck, such as a drill chuck, which can be held on its Morse taper in the headstock. This smaller chuck allows more movement around the work when turning the fine details.

Prepare all the blanks in the following manner:

1 Hold the square blank in the chuck, supporting the tailstock end with a revolving centre. Turn the work round. Reverse the piece in the lathe and turn the remaining square to round. At the tailstock end turn a 1/4in (6mm) diameter spigot 1/4in (6mm) long. This spigot is used to hold the work in the small drill chuck and will also act as a joint between the turned piece and the separately turned base.

1

The bases are cut using a 1¹/₂in (38mm) plug cutter. Plugs of this diameter are cut from prepared walnut and maple 4in (100mm) wide by ¹/₄in (6mm) thick. This seems the quickest and most efficient method of production.

The centre of each plug is discovered using a compass set to the radius of the plug. The point of the compass is placed on the edge of the plug and an arc is struck towards the centre. The point of the compass is moved to another position on the edge of the plug and a further arc is struck. Where the two arcs cross will be the centre of the plug. Alternatively, an engineer's centre finder could be used. At the centre of each plug, drill through using a ¹/₄in (6mm) drill.

2

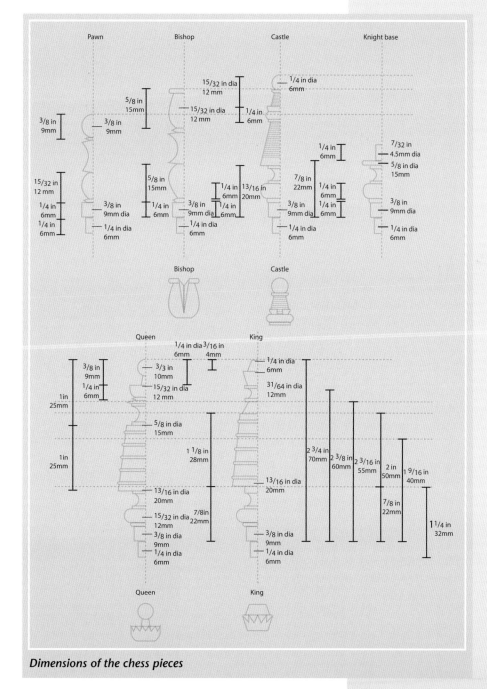

Dimensions of the chess pieces

Turning the shafts of the pieces

1 Hold the ¼in (6mm) spigot in the drill chuck set in the headstock. Support the other end with a revolving centre. Turn the piece true and to the major diameter of the chess piece being turned. Draw on card the shape of the piece, be it castle, knight stem, pawn, bishop, king or queen. With the lathe running, hold the template close to the revolving work. Transfer the major points from the template to the work.

1

2 The coves are turned using fine gouges and occasionally a small skew. The convex curves and beads are turned using a ¼in (6mm) skew chisel. Fine lines can be incised using the corner of a square end tool.

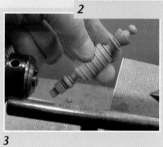

2

3 When the piece has been fully turned and sanded to a good finish (don't sand out fine details) it may be polished and parted off.

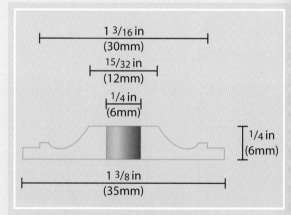

3

Turning the Bases

1 For the dimensions of the bases, see the illustration. Fit a piece of wood to the faceplate and turn its face flat and true. Drill a ¼in (6mm) hole centrally through the wood. Fit and glue ¼in (6mm) dowel at its centre so that 5mm (³⁄₁₆in) is showing.

Take a plug cut disc with the drilled hole at its centre and apply pieces of double-sided sticky tape to its underside, then press the hole on the taped side over the dowel down and onto the wood faceplate. Turn the outer edge to a true 1³⁄₈in (35mm) diameter.

1 3/16 in
(30mm)

15/32 in
(12mm)

1/4 in
(6mm)

1/4 in
(6mm)

1 3/8 in
(35mm)

1 A cross-section of the base for the chess pieces

2 Using light cuts (don't forget that the piece is only held with sticky tape), turn to shape then polish. Remove from the dowel and move on to the next base.

2

Finishing Touches

1 Once all the bases have been turned, carry out the finishing touches to the chess pieces. Cut the crenellations in the castle, the segments in the king's and queen's crowns and the mitre in the top of the bishop. These cut sections are simply produced. Use a junior hacksaw to make the preparatory cuts, having marked the positions of the special cut sections. The hacksaw cuts can be widened out using a small needle file or triangular file.

1

2 When cutting and cleaning these areas, fix masking tape to the surrounding parts where the saw or file may stray and cause damage. It is better to mark a piece of masking tape, which can be removed and replaced, than to mark the chess piece.

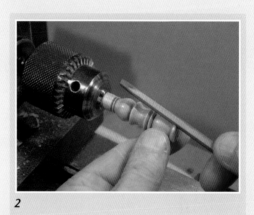

2

3 Drill into the underside of the knight, centrally of course, to take the stem and fit to the base. Fit all the remaining pieces to their bases to complete the fully turned chess set. The knight may be carved (I find it easier to use a dental burr in a flexible drive) to produce the more recognizable features, or it may be left plain. The choice is yours.

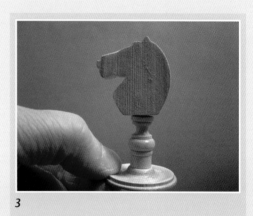

3

CHAPTER 7

STREPTOHEDRONS

STREPTOHEDRONS

In June 2001 I was sent two interesting turned pieces. One was a turned cone – its cross-section was an equal sided triangle – which had been split vertically from the point to the centre of the base. The two halves had then been rotated so that the edge of one half-cone lay against the base of the other half-cone. (See the picture overleaf.) The two halves had then been glued together to produce a form which has only one side and one edge.

The second piece was in the form of two cones fixed base to base. Its cross-section appeared to be a diamond shape. Again this had been split centrally from point to point, with one half rotated through 90 degrees before being glued to the other to create a form with one side and two edges. This piece called to mind the Mobius strip, a narrow strip of paper given one twist and joined at its ends to produce a piece of paper with only one side. The twisted double cone rolls drunkenly down a slope, while the twisted single cone also rolls in a bizarre manner but stops at one of the half-bases. I remembered another similar form produced by Hans Weissflog some eight years earlier. It was in the shape of a thin cylinder with a disc at its centre which, when it was split and one half was rotated through 90 degrees before being re-glued, produced another unusual twisted form.

Twisted double cone

Twisted pentagon

Twisted hexagon cross-section

I discovered that the double cone led back to an article in the *Scientific American*, October 1999, by Professor Ian Stewart, who had explained that C.J Roberts first developed the twisted double cone in 1969, calling it a sphericon. The many variations of turned, split, twisted and re-joined forms I have developed from this basic idea I have called streptohedrons (twisted polygons).

I now looked more closely at the shapes I had: a twisted cone, a twisted double cone and a twisted cylinder/disc. They had no apparent link, except that they were solids of rotation and their cross-sections were symmetrical about a centre line, these being a triangle, a diamond and a cross.

But I had been looking at the diamond cross-section the wrong way, it was a square rotated through its points, and that was the breakthrough. A triangle (three sides), a square (four sides) . . . What next? A pentagon, of course, (five sides), followed by a hexagon (six sides).

Now I will show you how to turn these forms based upon regular polygons (triangle, square, pentagon and hexagon each, individually, having sides which are the same length). These basic forms are intriguing shapes when complete, but their real value is as a stepping stone in understanding how they are made. This will enable you to move on to other, more complex forms. The sizes given for each of the shapes below will enable you to turn without having to decide on sizes for yourself. As you become more proficient I would hope that you will produce your own drawings with your own sizes.

A cone split, twisted and rejoined to form a conicon

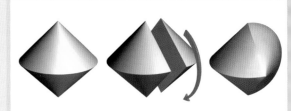

A double cone split, twisted and rejoined to form a sphericon

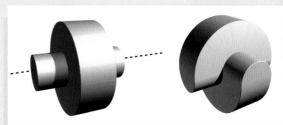

A piece with a cross-shaped section split, twisted and rejoined

Important Points when Preparing and Turning Streptohedrons

The most important starting point is to produce an accurate drawing of the shape that you are about to turn. To learn how to draw these shapes please see Chapter 3: Drawing Shapes.

The blank needs to be prepared the day before, turning using a newspaper/glue joint. See Chapter 2 for instructions.

The prepared blank is first turned between centres. The driving dog and the revolving cup centre must be located exactly on the glue line of the blank, see Chapter 2. For details of safe turning of newspaper/glue blanks see also Chapter 2.

If you decide to skip the first section and move on to turning star shapes, for example, it is still important that you read through this whole section first to gain an understanding of the methods used to turn accurate points, valleys and slopes.

For those who work with imperial measurements: As the imperial dimensions on the drawings provided are translated from the metric it is advisable to prepare accurate drawings in inches and use those measurements when turning these streptohedrons.

Accurate Turning

No doubt one or two who are reading this will think, 'I cannot turn that accurately'. Do not be concerned, you most probably have already turned accurately without knowing. Have you turned a round tenon for a chair or a stool? If so, you have turned accurately. If the tenon is too big it will not fit. If it is too small it will fall out. Have you turned a dovetail on the base of a bowl blank so that it may be held in the dovetail recess of a chuck? If so you have turned accurately. Have you turned a lid for a box? If so, you have turned sufficiently accurately. Have you turned and successfully used a jam chuck? If so, you have turned accurately.

Do you remember those dot-to-dot drawings where you joined the numbered dots with a pencil to produce a face, an animal or a flower? Well, to turn accurately you only have to join the dots. That's where the drawing becomes so useful. It provides the start and finish points of the cut you need to make. Just join the dots and the shape appears.

Directions

Turning points: See pages 69 and 85.

Turning valleys, side and end: See pages 84 and 90.

Turning legs: See pages 104–5.

Tip

These pieces and any following streptohedrons may also be turned elliptically. Hybrids, part elliptical and part round, will provide unusual results.

The Twisted Cone

1 Draw out an equal sided triangle with 70mm (2³/₄in) sides (see Chapter 3). This will provide the diameter of the piece and the positions of point A (at the apex of the cone) and point B (on the base circumference of the cone).

From your chosen wood (I am using padauk), cut two lengths 4in (100mm) long by 3in (75mm) wide by 1¹/₂in (38mm) thick, each planed flat on one side. Glue them together with a newspaper/glue joint, planed side to planed side, so that a 3in (75mm) square blank is produced. When the glue has dried, turn the blank to a cylinder as described in Chapter 2.

Hold the blank in a chuck, accurately relocating the cup centre in the marked point at the tailstock end. Turn to an accurate 2³/₄in (70mm) diameter.

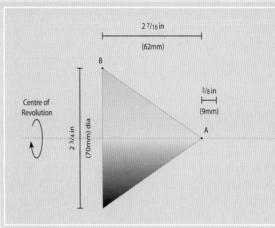

1 Triangular cross-section with equal length sides

2 From the tailstock end measure ³/₈in (9mm) and mark with a pencil line, line A. (Point A in the diagram will be directly below this line.) From that line measure towards the headstock 2⁷/₁₆in (62mm), marking a second pencil line, line B. (Point B will be directly below this line.)

2

3 On the tailstock side of line A turn down to ¹/₂in (12mm) diameter. As this section is waste wood, the hollow created by the cup centre can eventually be turned away. On the headstock side of line B turn down to about 1⁵/₈in (40mm) diameter. Begin by turning a slope from the headstock down towards the tailstock, stopping short of line B. The angle of the slope can be checked by comparing the unturned diameter at point A to the unturned area from B to the start of the slope. If they are the same then the slope is at the correct angle. If not, make adjustments to the slope so they match.

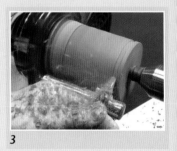

3

4 When most of the slope has been turned, but still stopping short of line B, the waste wood on the tailstock side of line A can be turned away.

5 Now the sloping side of the cone can be completed. Just join point A, which is the centre point of the work at the tailstock end, with point B, the rim of the base of the cone. The side of the cone must be straight and flat.

6 The diameter of the base is equal to the length of the side of the cone. Check this measurement before parting off. Adjustments may still be made. Sand and polish the turned cone.

7 Skim the base with the tip of a skew chisel and continue to part off using a fine parting tool.

8 If you are unhappy about parting the cone fully, then stop when a small, turned diameter remains and saw off the stub. But be careful not to allow the saw to mark the rim of the base. The photograph shows the parted-off cone. The base may be sanded flat but, again, be careful to keep the base flat and do not sand into the edges.

Splitting the newspaper/glue joint

1 As the glue line is quite thin, care must be taken when splitting this joint line. To avoid breaking into the wood, on either side of the line, use a craft knife to start the cut. Place the blade accurately on the glue line and tap with a hammer.

Once the glue line has been slightly opened with the craft knife, replace it with a less sharp kitchen knife.

This blunt knife will act a wedge, forcing the joint open. If the blunt knife was used first it would damage the area around the newspaper/glue joint.

1

2 The two halves have now been separated.

2

3 The half-cones can be joined to give a left or a right hand twist. Try the left or right twist before gluing the parts together.

All that remains is to sand the newspaper from the flat, split faces and glue the halves together, having remembered to twist one half before joining. Use masking tape to hold the two together while the glue dries. Do not be dismayed if the two halves do not match accurately, this is your first attempt. When the pieces are glued together and have dried, the joint can be sanded to produce a smooth form.

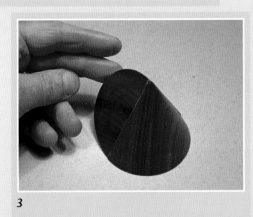

3

4 The finished piece.

4

Turning an accurate point

Turning an accurate point on a cone is straightforward. Having produced the drawing, turned the blank to size and found the start and finish points of the cone, it is just a case of joining the dots. Once the supporting waste wood has been removed and the tailstock withdrawn, the end of the cone is free and open, allowing a clear view of the end point.

Turning the double cone is much the same, but at the headstock end the point of the cone is buried within the supporting wood. Because there is no open end here to help you locate the exact position of the end point, you must use an interim finish point which will be located somewhere along the sloping side. When the slope of this side has been established it can be continued and the apex parted off.

The position of an interim finish point must first be located on the drawing that you have made. In the illustration below, for example, place a rule along the diameter of the drawn shape (line A) and, keeping the rule parallel to that line, slide it along until you have a convenient whole number of units between the two sloping sides. This can be seen as lines C and D, 3/4in (20mm) diameter, on this diagram.

All that remains is to turn a slope from point A to point C and from point A to point D. This will establish the correct angled slopes which can eventually be continued to the end points. This principle can be used wherever a finish point is located in essential supporting wood.

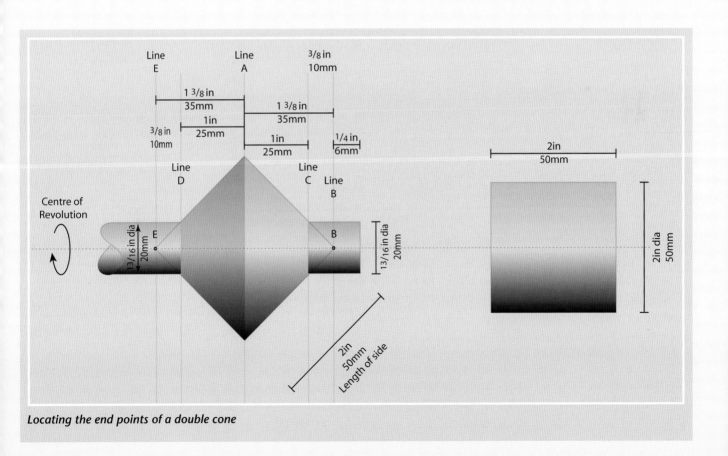

Locating the end points of a double cone

The Twisted Double Cone

This double cone is a wonderful shape to produce and the resulting split, twisted and re-glued form, the sphericon, is fun to watch as it drunkenly rolls down a slope. Although it appears difficult to turn, because it has a point at either end, it really is quite easy when taken simple step by simple step.

Twisted double cone

1 First make an accurate drawing of the cross-section of the work, or use the drawing provided. Prepare the blank, as before, from two pieces of 4in (100mm) long by 3in (75mm) wide by 1½in (38mm) thick hardwood, gluing the two parts together, with a newspaper/glue joint, to produce a 3in (75mm) square blank. Allow a day for the glue to dry before turning it to a cylinder.

Hold the rounded blank in a chuck, relocating the cup centre in the marked point at the tailstock end, and turn to an accurate 2¾in (70mm) diameter.

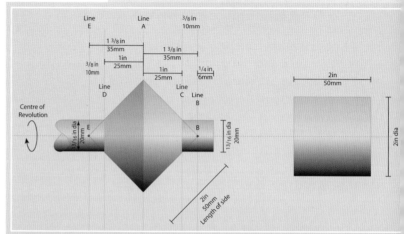

1 *Squares with centre of revolution through points and flats*

2 From the tailstock end mark pencil lines at the following positions: ¼in (6mm), for line B; from that line measure ¹³/₃₂in (10mm) for line C; from that line measure 1in (25mm) and mark line A. From line A, towards the headstock, measure 1in (25mm) and mark line D; and finally measure from line D ¹³/₃₂in (10mm) towards the headstock to mark line E.

2

3 On the tailstock side of line B, turn down to 25mm (1in) diameter and between lines C and B turn to an accurate ¹³/₁₆in (20mm) diameter spigot. This locates intermediate point C.

3

4 On the headstock side of line D turn an accurate ¹³/₁₆in (20mm) diameter tenon. This locates intermediate point D.

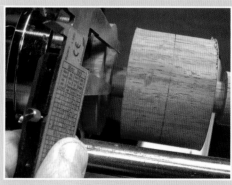

4

5 To turn the initial slope on the tailstock side of the centre line A, join up points A and C with a good, straight cut. I am most comfortable using my small skew to turn the intermediate slope. A gouge will work just as well. Choose the tool which works for you.

6 As a guide, when turning the slope, look carefully at the distances between the cut produced and the start point and then the cut produced and the finish point.

7 If these two distances are the same then the angle is correct and you may confidently continue turning the slope. If the distances differ, then alter the angle of the cut so that those two distances are equal and continue when satisfied that the angle is correct.

8 Continue the cut until point A is joined to point C.

9 Next turn the slope on the headstock side of line A. Continue the cut until point A is joined to point D.

10 The two part-turned slopes.

11 To complete the slope at the tailstock end, turn away the ¼in (6mm) waste wood closest to the cup centre then withdraw the tailstock. This will leave the end position B open so that the slope can be turned down to a point. Sand and polish both slopes.

11

12 Having established the angle of the slope, follow through with parting cuts at the headstock end to produce a point. A double cone will have been turned.

12

13 It is not necessary to part off the point cleanly. If a little stub remains, as long as the point is contained within that stub, the point may be trimmed using a sharp knife. Sand and polish to match the whole turned piece.

13

Turning an accurate tenon

The trick to turning an accurate tenon is to turn on the waste side of the area allocated for that spigot. For example: the waste side of line D is closest to the headstock and there is at least 1in (25mm) available. So turn down to¹³/₁₆in (20mm) close to the headstock first.

If the cut is accurate then turn closer to line D using that first cut as a guide. If you turn too small that too acts as a guide, you still have enough wood left to turn closer to line D. Make adjustments until the correct size is achieved then turn all the way up to line D.

Splitting the newspaper/glue joint

1. To make the initial opening of the glue line take a craft knife, place the blade on the join line and tap with a hammer. Use a blunt kitchen knife to open up the joint line.

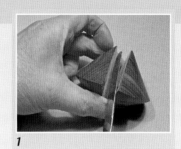

2. When opened, the square cross-section can be seen. Now clean off the newspaper/glue residue from the split faces and glue the two halves together, remembering to twist one half through 90°. Use masking tape to hold the halves together whilst the glue dries. Here the two parts have been twisted and temporarily rejoined.

The Twisted Cylinder

1. If a square cross-section is rotated on its points, a double cone is produced. But take that same square cross-section and rotate it through the centre of the flats and a cylinder is produced. If the cylinder is split along the newspaper/ glue line and the halves twisted then rejoined then a rather uninteresting form is produced.

2. The curved outer edge is similar to the seam line around a tennis ball.

3. This picture shows the square cross-section and profiles of both forms. But you will notice that the square cross-section of each is exactly the same size so the half of one can be joined with one half of the other to produce a hybrid form.

4. Hybrids can only be produced by mixing the halves of equal-sided streptohedrons: square (4), hexagon (6), octagon (8), etc. What happens to those with an odd number of sides I will explain shortly. As turning a cylinder is such a basic technique, I will leave it to those of you who are interested in producing either the square hybrid or the twisted cylinder to work it out by yourselves.

The Pentagon

Twisted pentagon

1 First make an accurate drawing of the pentagon (see Chapter 3) or work from the drawing provided. Prepare the blank, as before, from two pieces of 4in (100mm) long by 3in (75mm) wide by 1½in (38mm) thick hardwood, gluing the two parts together with a newspaper/glue joint to produce a blank 3in (75mm) square. Allow a day for the glue to dry before turning it to a cylinder.

Hold the rounded blank in a chuck, relocating the cup centre in the marked point at the tailstock end, and turn to an accurate 2¾in (70mm) diameter. From the tailstock end measure ⅜in (9mm) and mark a pencil line, line B. From line B, measure towards the headstock 1in (25mm) and mark pencil line A. From line A, measure towards the headstock 1⅝in (41mm) and mark pencil line C.

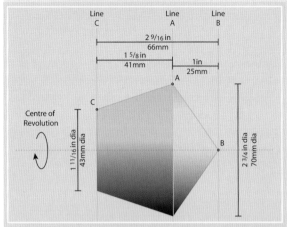

1 *Pentagon cross-section*

2 On the tailstock side of line B, turn down to 1in (25mm).

2

3 On the headstock side of line C, turn down to an accurate 1⅝in (43mm) diameter.

3

4 Now join point C to point A with a straight cut. This is just dot-to-dot turnery.

4

5 It is quite deceptive. The length of the side looks much larger than the diameter at C...

6 ...But check the sizes and you will see that they are the same.

7 Now turn the waste wood away from the tailstock side of line B.

8 Dot-to-dot turnery again, join point A to point B.

9 Here I am using my favourite small skew chisel, a larger skew or a gouge would work equally well.

10 Check the length of the side against the diameter at C...

10

11 ...and the side AC. Begin parting off the base. Remember to trim the base crisply with the nose of a skew. Before parting off, polish the work. Now part off the completed pentagon.

11

12 If you are happy to support the work with your hand whilst parting through, fine, but if you are uncertain of this technique the small remaining spigot can be sawn through, remembering to avoid marking the base. The base can be sanded flat on a sheet of abrasive paper supported on a flat surface. Remember to keep the work flat on the abrasive paper. Split the newspaper/glue joint using first a craft knife then a blunt kitchen knife.

12

13 The picture shows the pentagonal cross-section of the split piece. These forms with an odd number of sides (excluding three) when twisted and rejoined will produce more than one shape, but hybrids cannot be made from these odd-sided forms.

13

14 When twisting the two halves of a pentagon, the point of one half can be aligned with the edge of the other to produce one shape...

14

15 ...Or the point of one half of the pentagon can be aligned with the base of the other half to produce a different twisted shape. A heptagon (seven-sided) streptohedron will have three different alignments and a nonagon (nine-sided) streptohedron will have four different alignments – plus, of course, left and right hand alignments for all.

15

The Hexagon (Centre of revolution through the points)

1 First make an accurate drawing of the hexagon (see Chapter 3) or work from the drawing provided. Prepare the blank, as before, from two pieces of 4in (100mm) long by 3in (75mm) wide by 1½in (38mm) thick hardwood, gluing the two parts together with a newspaper/glue joint to make a 3in (75mm) square blank. Allow a day for the glue to dry before turning it round. Hold the rounded blank in a chuck, relocating the cup centre in the marked point at the tailstock end and turn to an accurate 2⁷⁄₁₆in (61mm) diameter. See illustration.

Hexagon

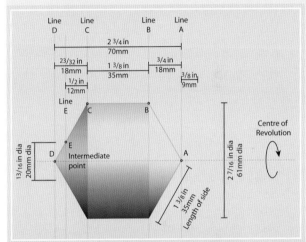

1 Hexagon with centre of revolution through the points

2 From the tailstock end measure ³⁄₈in (9mm) and mark a pencil line, line A. From line A measure and mark a pencil line ³⁄₄in (18mm) away, towards the headstock, to locate line B. From line B measure and mark a pencil line, towards the headstock, 1³⁄₈in (35mm) away to locate line C. From line C measure and mark a pencil line ³⁄₄in (18mm), towards the headstock, to locate line D. On the tailstock side of line A, initially turn down to 1⁹⁄₁₆in (40mm).

2

3 On the headstock side of line D, turn down to 1⁹⁄₁₆in (40mm). Return to line A and now turn away all the wood on the tailstock side of line A. Withdraw the tailstock.

3

4 The start position for the sloping cut, the top of line B, and the finish position, the centre of the blank point A, can now be seen.

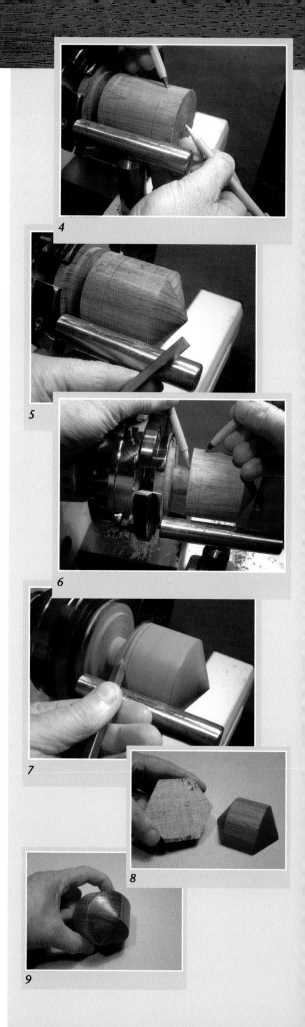

5 All that remains is to join those two points with a clean, straight cut. Dot-to-dot turnery. To turn the point at position D an interim point, E, will have to be located between C and D. Refer to Turning an Accurate Point on pages 69 and 85. To locate line E, from line C measure and mark a pencil line ½in (12mm) towards the headstock. On the headstock side of line E, turn down to an accurate $^{13}/_{16}$ in (20mm) diameter.

6 Now join point C to interim point E...

7 ...with a clean, straight cut. Sand and polish the part-finished piece. Having established the angle at the headstock end, follow through at that same angle with parting cuts to produce the point at D. If a small unturned end remains attached to point D, gently trim it away using a sharp knife as seen on page 72.

8 The newspaper/glue joint may now be split and the halves opened to reveal the hexagonal cross-section.

9 The two halves can be twisted and temporarily rejoined to form the intriguing new shape. This new form can have a right or a left-handed twist. Clean the newspaper from the joint surface by rubbing on a flat sheet of abrasive paper.

The Hexagon (Centre of revolution through the flats)

There are two centres of rotation upon which a hexagon may be revolved, through the points or through the flats (see the pictures, right). I will now describe how to turn a piece with a hexagonal cross-section with the centre of rotation through the flats.

Twisted hexagon

Rotation through the points

1 First make an accurate drawing of the hexagon (see Chapter 3) or work from the drawing provided. Prepare the blank, as before, from two pieces of 4in (100mm) long by 3in (75mm) wide by 1½in (38mm) thick hardwood, gluing the two parts together with a newspaper/glue joint to produce a 3in (75mm) square blank. Allow a day for the glue to dry before turning it to a cylinder.

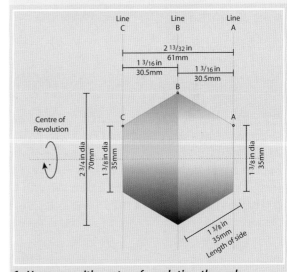

1 Hexagon with centre of revolution through the flats

Hold the rounded blank in a chuck, relocating the cup centre in the marked point at the tailstock end and turn to an accurate 2¾in (70mm) diameter. From the tailstock end measure ½in (12mm) and mark a pencil line A. From line A measure 1³/₁₆in (30.5mm) towards the headstock to locate and mark line B.

Rotation through the flats

2 From line B measure 1³/₁₆in (30.5mm) towards the headstock to locate and mark line C. On the tailstock side of line A turn an accurate 1³/₈in (35mm) diameter spigot. On the headstock side of line C do the same.

2

3 The start and finish points of the sloping sides have now been located, so join point B to point A with a clean, straight cut.

3

4 Measure the sloping side, it should be exactly 1³/₈in (35mm) long, the same as the spigots turned at either end. These spigots determine the length of the hexagon side located at the ends.

4

5 Now turn the sloping side from point B to point C. When this side is measured it should be 1³/₈in (35mm), the same as the spigots at either end. Sand and polish the piece before parting off on the tailstock side of line A. Remember to skim the end with the point of a skew to provide a crisp finish. Part off on the headstock side of line C, remembering to skim the end with the skew to provide a crisp finish.

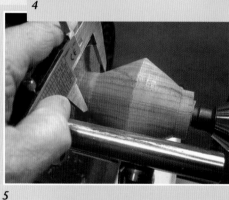

5

6 The piece may now be split to reveal the hexagonal cross-section. Then it can be twisted and temporarily rejoined. This twisted form can have either a left hand twist or a right hand twist.

6

Hybrids

I hope that you will have noticed that the two hexagonal cross-section pieces, although turned on different axes, have the same 'footprint'. They will have the same length of side 1⅜in (35mm). So take half of the first hexagon that was turned (pages 77-78) and fit it against a half of the second hexagon (pages 79-80).

They will fit together to produce a hybrid form. The picture shows all the split sections of all the streptohedrons produced so far.

Fitting the Halves

If the shapes that you have just completed are to be joined, either as hybrids or in their regular form, some adjustment may be needed to make the curves flow into one another, particularly in the early stages of turning when practice with accuracy is necessary. As an example I will show how to fit two hexagonal halves together.

1

To clean the newspaper/glue from the split surface, first place a sheet of glasspaper upon a flat surface. Rub the split face of the hexagon upon the glasspaper.

2

When both faces have been cleaned, apply a moderate amount of glue to both surfaces. Rub the two faces together to help the glue grip and line up the edges as closely as possible.

Apply masking tape to the edges to hold the two halves together whilst the glue sets.

3

Important

Let's be realistic about this, it is not always the case that every shape turned will be perfectly accurate, particularly those first attempts; so when the glued piece has dried, carefully sand or file the edges until they flow into one another.

This will only work with slight to moderate misalignments. If the edges are too far out then use the experience you have just gained and start again. The finished work may be textured if you wish, but do not use texturing to hide bad work.

CHAPTER 8

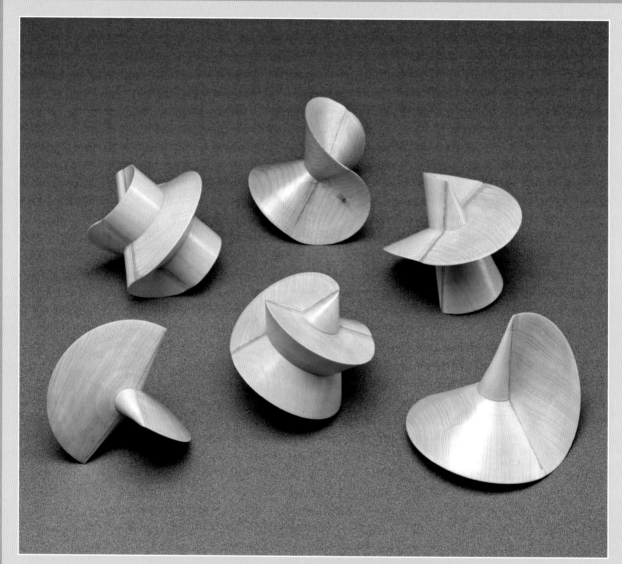

STAR-SHAPED STREPTOHEDRONS

STAR-SHAPED STREPTOHEDRONS

Having worked through the regular polygons, it suddenly struck me that I could experiment with other shapes as long as they were regularly formed, so that when rotated their cross-sections would match. (They would have rotational symmetry.) Star shapes seemed to be the natural progression and for some reason the five-pointed star was the first I tried. The resultant twisted form was stunning, from then on I was hooked.

To make it easier to understand how these shapes can be turned I will begin by describing how to turn two particular parts whilst producing a three point star. They are: valleys in the ends of the turned forms and long, slender points. As before, it's dot-to-dot turnery. All you need to know are the positions of the start and finish points, then all that is required is to join them. Always begin with an accurate drawing.

A Three-Pointed Star

Here I am using castello boxwood because I need a wood which is strong enough to hold a very thin edge without breaking out. Prepare the blank, as before, from two pieces of 4in (100mm) long by 3³/₁₆in (80mm) wide by 1¹⁹/₃₂in (40mm) thick hardwood, gluing the two parts together with a newspaper/glue joint to produce an 3³/₁₆ in (80mm) square blank. Allow a day for the glue to dry before turning it to a cylinder. Hold the rounded blank in a chuck, relocating the cup centre in the marked point at the tailstock end and turn to an accurate 2¹⁵/₁₆in (74mm) diameter. Face off the end square and true.

Three-pointed star

Turning an end valley

1 Cut from card a template, indicating the diameter and depth needed to provide the correct internal shape. The photo shows the card template. Also shown in the photograph is a tool which has been specially ground from high carbon tool steel.

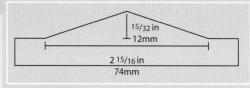

Card template

1

2 This will slice into the end grain and, provided it is kept sharp, will cut cleanly. Notice that the tool angle is aligned with the pointed template end. Typist correction fluid is used to make a mark in line with the pencil mark indicating the entrance to the valley. This white mark on the tool, if it is kept parallel to the end grain face, will keep the tool at the correct angle.

2 *Specially ground slicing tool*

3 Use a shelf toolrest to support the tool which will be cutting at centre height (this provides great support for the tool, preventing it from being dragged into the work). Gently slice into the end-grain face to produce the required slope.

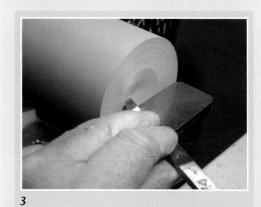

3

4 Check regularly with the card template to ensure that the angle is correct and make adjustments where necessary. In conjunction with the card template the white mark on the tool will help indicate when the correct depth has been reached. Sand and polish the end valley. The end valley has now been turned. Other end valleys are turned in a similar way. Support the completed end valley with a turned plug between it and the revolving centre.

4

5

5 A small piece of cloth will prevent the wood plug from marking the end valley. Do not be tempted to use the revolving centre in the end valley without the supporting plug because firstly it will mark the end valley with a deep point and secondly the centre can more easily act as a wedge and split open the newspaper/glue joint. The edge of the end face is now line A. Measure 1^{1}/$_{32}$in (26mm) from A towards the headstock to locate position B. From line B measure 1^{9}/$_{16}$in (39mm) towards the headstock to locate position D. On the headstock side of line B, turn down to ^{11}/$_{16}$in (17mm) diameter.

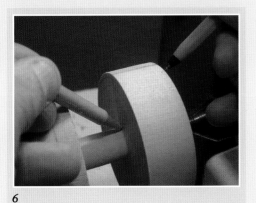

6

6 The start and finish points of the sloping side AB are known, so join those two points with a clean, sloping cut. Then sand and polish the slope.

Preparing a long, slender point

Refer to the drawing for the start and finish positions of the long, slender point.

The start position, B, is known at ^{11}/$_{16}$in (17mm) diameter. The finish position, D, is known at 0ins (0mm) diameter, a point, 1^{9}/$_{16}$in (39mm) away from A. **BUT** it is not so easy just to join the dots and part off in one go, so use the drawing to establish an intermediary point, C somewhere along the slender point which when joined to B will create the correct slope. That slope can then be continued and the point parted off.

On the drawing of the slender point slide the rule along, parallel, from the ^{11}/$_{16}$in (17mm) start point at B, until a convenient diameter is found. In this case it is ^{3}/$_{8}$in (10mm) diameter, which is ^{5}/$_{8}$in (15mm) away from B.

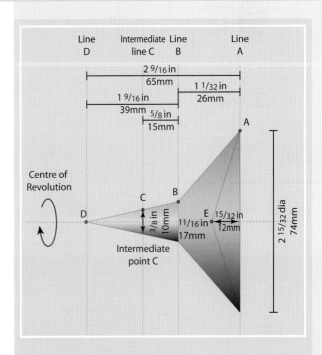

Turning the long, slender point

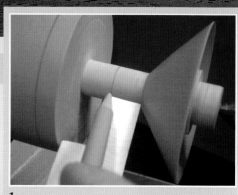

1

1 First turn the whole length, which will eventually be the long point, to $^{11}/_{16}$in (17mm) diameter by $1^9/_{16}$in (39mm) long. Point C is marked $^5/_8$in (15mm) away from B.

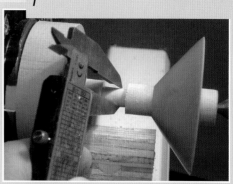

2

2 On the headstock side of line C, turn down to $^3/_8$in (10mm) diameter.

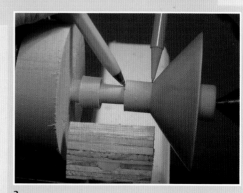

3

3 B and C must now be joined with a straight cut to produce the correct angle of the long point.

4 Continue the angled cut finishing at D. Polish before parting off.

4

5 Now carefully split the newspaper/glue joint by placing a craft knife on the joint and lightly tapping with a hammer to reveal the three-pointed star shape within. Clean off the newspaper/glue line, rotate one half and rejoin to produce a most elegant form.

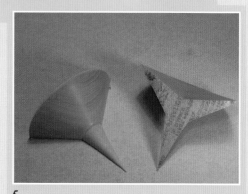

5

Turning a Four-Pointed Star (centre of rotation through the points)

1. Make an accurate, dimensioned drawing of the four-pointed star. Prepare the blank from two pieces each 4in (100mm) long by 3⁵/₃₂in (80mm) wide by 1⁹/₁₆ in (40mm) thick. Glue the two pieces together with a newspaper/glue joint so that the blank is now 3⁵/₃₂ in (80mm) square. Leave the glue to dry then turn to a cylinder, wasting as little diameter as possible. Here I am using castello boxwood. Hold the prepared blank in a chuck, supporting the tailstock end with a revolving cup centre, and turn to an accurate 2¹⁵/₁₆in (74mm) diameter.

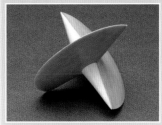

Twisted Four-Pointed Star

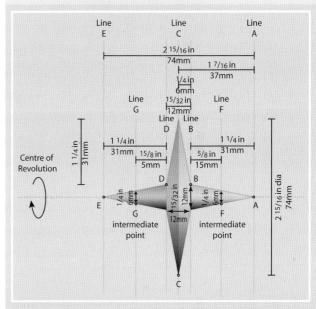

1 Four-pointed star

2. Moving from the tailstock end of the turned blank towards the headstock, mark a series of pencil lines. The first line is set ³/₈in (9mm) from the end to mark line A. From line A measure 1¹/₄in (31mm) to mark line B, followed by ¹/₄in (6mm) to mark line C, then a further ¹/₄in (6mm) for line D and finally, from line D, measure another 1¹/₄in (31mm) to mark line E. Use a parting tool to turn the area between lines A and B to an accurate ¹/₂in (12mm) diameter. Now move to the other side of line D and turn the area between lines D and E to an accurate ¹/₂in (12mm). Turn from line C down to where line B touches the ¹/₂in (12mm) turned area with a straight, clean cut to produce one angled face.

2

3. Turn the angled face on the opposite side of C down to where line D touches the ¹/₂in (12mm) area. For those who do not wish to use a skew, a parting tool can be used as shown here – but the tool has to be kept very sharp to prevent tearing out the grain. When satisfied with the two cut faces, sand and polish.

3

4 From the base of the angled face closest to the tailstock, measure ⅝in (15mm) towards the tailstock, and mark this position with a pencil, F. As it is difficult for a rule to be used in such a tight space, transfer the measurement to a piece of card and use that as a guide.

4

5 On the tailstock side of line F, turn down to an accurate ¼in (6mm). A temporary wood toolrest can be seen in the photograph. This provides support to the parting tool close to the work. Now join the dots. Turn a slope from line B to the ¼in (6mm) diameter at line F. This will provide the correct angle for the long, slender point. Continue this same angle towards the tailstock end, but do not cut too thin just yet.

5

6 Repeat the whole process on the opposite side, marking line G, ⅝in (15mm) away from line D towards the headstock, then turning down to ¼in (6mm) diameter on the headstock side. Join those points to produce an accurate slope, continue that slope towards the headstock to produce the required slender point. Again stop short of parting off. Sand and polish each point. If either point has been turned too thin, then the twisting force on those points, created as the lathe rotates, can twist the point off leaving a jagged, useless end, so beware.

6

7 Now gently part off each end. I usually leave a small block on the end of each point and saw off on the waste side of that block. This prevents a damaged, twisted point. The ends can be trimmed to shape using a craft knife. Use a craft knife to begin splitting the newspaper/glue joint and then a less sharp dinner knife to finally wedge the joint apart.

7

Turn a Four-Pointed Star (centre of revolution through the valleys)

1 Make an accurate, dimensioned drawing of the four-pointed star with the rotational centre through the valleys. Prepare the blank from two pieces each 4in (100mm) long by 2³/₈in (60mm) wide by 1³/₁₆in (30mm) thick. Glue them together with a newspaper/glue joint so the blank will now be 2³/₈in (60mm) square. Leave the glue to dry then turn to a cylinder, wasting as little diameter as possible. Here I am using maple.

Hold the prepared blank in a chuck, supporting the tailstock end with revolving cup centre, and turn to an accurate 2¹/₁₆in (52mm) diameter. An end valley will be turned into the end face, so begin by turning the end face flat and true. Have available the slicing tool described on page 84 and also have ready a shelf toolrest.

2 Prepare a card template to the shape of the end valley. This will be a vee-shape 2¹/₁₆in (52mm) wide at the base and ²³/₃₂in (18mm) high at its midpoint.

3 Set the slicing tool on the card template with its point aligned with the template point. Use typists' correction fluid to mark a line on the tool matching the base line of the template. This thick white line will act as a guide when slicing into the end face.

4 Set the shelf toolrest so that the tool cuts at centre height. Hold the tool so the white line is parallel to the face of the work. Make a series of light, slicing cuts to begin the shaping of the end valley. Regularly check the turned hollow, making adjustments where necessary. Keep the slicing tool sharp to ensure a clean cut. Use the white mark to help judge the depth of the cut as well as a guide to the angle of the cut. When satisfied, sand and polish. For the next stage, support the end valley with a turned plug. Place a small piece of cloth between the plug and the work to prevent marking.

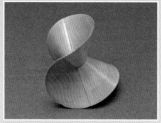

Twisted four-pointed star

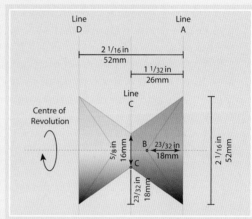

1 Four-pointed star with centre of revolution through the valleys

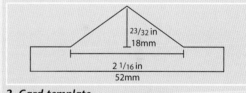

2 Card template

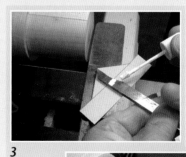

3

4

Turning the side valley

The method described to turn the side valley in this four-pointed star can also be used when working similar shapes on other streptohedrons.

Draw two card templates, the first is vee-shaped to show the full width and depth of the valley and the second, half template, is shaped to show half of the width and the full depth of the valley. From the tailstock end (line A) measure, towards the headstock, 1¹/₃₂in (26mm) marking a pencil line at this point. This will be line C, the centre of the side valley. From this centre line measure a further 1¹/₃₂in (26mm) and mark another pencil line, line D. This is the end point of the valley and, in this case, the end of the four-pointed star. Make a small, vertical cut on line C. This will provide a stop for the slicing cuts yet to be made.

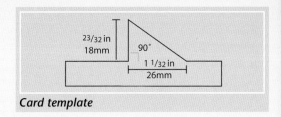

23/32 in
18mm
90°
1 1/32 in
26mm

Card template

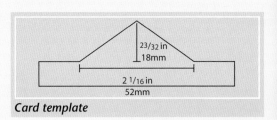

23/32 in
18mm
2 1/16 in
52mm

Card template

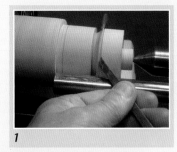

1

1 Slice, from the right, into that vertical cut (line C). Check the angle of the cut regularly using the half-template, making adjustments where necessary to ensure the slope is at the correct angle.

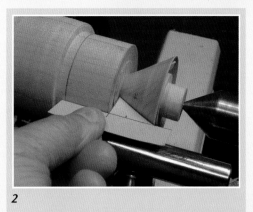

2

2 Continue the cut until the correct half-profile is achieved. The slope must start at the marked pencil line on the right and finish at the correct depth.

3

3 Next slice from the left, so that the pencil line on the left (line D) joins the base of the vee. Use the full card template to check that the shape is correct. Sand and polish before moving on.

Completing the four-pointed star

1 On the headstock side of line D, carefully turn in and part off. The blank now has a side valley and one end valley, with the second end valley waiting to be turned.

2 Screw an 8in (200mm) diameter by 1in (25mm) thick softwood disc to a faceplate. This will be used to hold the blank in conjunction with four shaped softwood supports. These softwood supports are shaped to fit the side valley of the blank and are screwed to the softwood disc, holding the blank firmly in place. To ensure that the blank runs centrally, first measure the diameter of the end valley. This should be 2¹/₁₆in (52mm). Mark this size, centrally, on the softwood disc. On the inside of this pencil circle turn a shallow groove. Test-fit the blank into the groove.

3 It should be a good, tight fit.

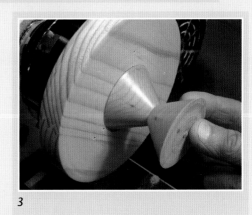

4 Use the revolving centre to hold the blank against the softwood disc and, importantly, on centre. Fit the shaped softwood supports around the blank and screw them firmly in place. To make sure that the blank does not move, apply dabs of hot-melt glue between the supports and the blank. Before the final dabs of hot-melt glue are applied, turn the lathe on to make sure that the piece runs truly on centre. Make adjustment where necessary by placing small strips of veneer between the supports and the blank. As the blank has a polished surface the hot melt will grip the work but will be easy to remove. Withdraw the tailstock and bring the shelf toolrest forward. Set the toolrest so that the slicing tool cuts at centre height.

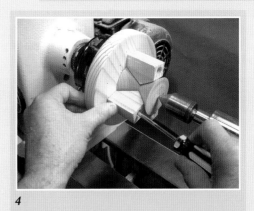

5 Rotate the lathe by hand to make sure nothing catches, then switch the lathe on. The white mark, still on the tool, will help set the cutting edge at the correct angle. Slice into the end face. Be careful of those ghost images whirling round. Keep your hands and fingers away. Use the card template regularly to check the turned hollow and make adjustments where necessary.

5

6 Continue turning into the end face and check, using the template, until the hollow is the exact shape of the template. Sand and polish the hollow.

6

7 Unscrew the supports to remove the finished piece. The dabs of hot-melt glue easily come away from the polished surface.

7

8 Using a craft knife, carefully split the joint to reveal the four-point star profile within.

Once the inner faces have been cleaned up, one half of the piece is rotated through 90° against the other and glued in place. Alternatively, one half of this four-pointed star can be joined to one half of the previous four-pointed star (with centre of rotation through the points) to make what I consider a more attractive hybrid shape.

8

Turning a Five-Pointed Star

This is much easier than the previous shape, for it may be turned in one go without the need for reversing or any use of clever holding devices.

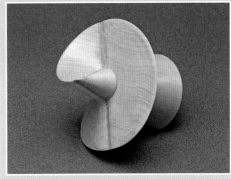

Twisted five-pointed star

1 Make an accurate, dimensioned drawing of the five-pointed star. Prepare the blank from two pieces each 4in (100mm) long by 3⁵/₃₂in (80mm) wide by 1⁹/₁₆in (40mm) thick. Glue them together with a newspaper/glue joint so that the blank will now be 3⁵/₃₂in (80mm) square. Leave the glue to dry then turn to a cylinder, wasting as little diameter as possible. Here I am using castello boxwood.

Hold the prepared blank in a chuck, supporting the tailstock end with the revolving cup centre, and turn to an accurate 2³/₄in (70mm) diameter. An end valley will be turned into the end face. Begin by turning the end face flat and true.

From the tailstock end, measure and mark a series of lines in pencil. Line 1 will be the start point, the edge at the tailstock end. Line 2 is set 1¹/₃₂in (26mm) away from the tailstock edge of the blank. From line 2 measure a further ⁵/₈in (15mm) and mark line 3. From line 3 measure 1in (25mm) and mark the final line, line 4.

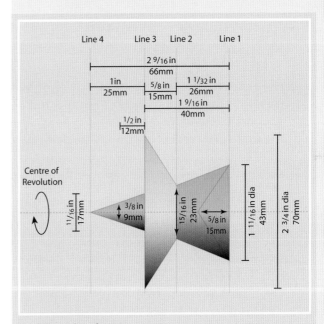

1 Five-pointed star

2 Withdraw the tailstock and mark on the end face a 1¹¹/₁₆in (43mm) diameter, concentric pencil circle.

2

3 Make a card template for the end valley as shown. Take the specially ground slicing tool (see page 84), make sure that it is sharp, and clean any white marks from its surface. Set the tool against the card template so that its tip is aligned with the point of the template. Then, using typists' correction fluid, make a mark which is in line with the base line on the template. Use a shelf toolrest to support the slicing tool and begin to cut into the end face to produce the end valley.

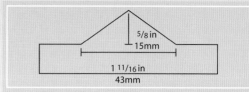

3 Card template

4 Regularly check the template in the turned hollow and make adjustments to the angle if necessary.

4

5 Here the shape of the tool is clearly seen. When satisfied with the shape of the end valley, sand and polish. To support the work fit a turned plug, with cloth buffer, into the end valley and bring the tailstock forward, pressing the centre into the marked hole in the plug. On the tailstock side of line 2, use a parting tool to turn down accurately to 1¹¹/₁₆in (43mm) diameter.

5

6 Cut a card template to the sizes shown in the illustration. This card template will help you judge the angle of the slope from line 1 down and towards line 2. Slice from line 1 down to ¹⁵/₁₆in (23mm) diameter at line 2. Constantly check with the template and make adjustments until the correct slope is achieved. The size may be cross-checked by measuring with callipers.

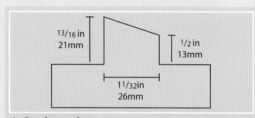

6 Card template

7 Now just join the dots. Join the top of line 3 with the base of line 2.

7

8

8 Using a parting tool, turn a fraction away from, and on the headstock side of, line 3. This will allow for the end-grain side of that line to be cleanly trimmed later. Turn that area down to $^{11}/_{16}$in (17mm) diameter. Check this size with a pair of callipers.

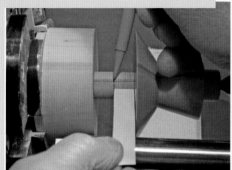

9

9 From the edge of line 3 measure $^1/_2$in (12mm) towards the headstock. The picture shows the measurement transferred from paper to the work. Carefully trim the vertical edge of line 3 using the nose of a skew. Turn away up to line 4 to make it easier to work. Sand and polish the two, now complete, sloping areas.

10

10 By checking on the drawing it will be noticed that at the point $^1/_2$in (12mm) away from line 3, recently marked in pencil, the diameter of the spike is $^3/_8$in (9mm). Now turn the area on the headstock side of this newly marked pencil line down to $^3/_8$in (9mm) diameter. Note that a small, temporary wood toolrest is being used to afford the tool close support. Measure the turned area to ensure that it is the correct diameter.

11

11 Turn the slope connecting the $^{11}/_{16}$in (17mm) diameter at line 3, with the $^3/_8$in (9mm) diameter area just turned. Continue to turn the slope, maintaining the angle, but do not part off. Sand and polish the spike and then carefully part off. As the lathe creates a twisting force it may be wise to cut the spike free, leaving plenty of waste wood on the headstock side. This can then be carefully shaped to a point using a sharp knife.

12

12 Carefully split the newspaper/glue joint and open to reveal the five-pointed star. Remember when gluing the two halves together there are choices: right or left hand twists and the point of one half may be brought to touch the edge of the other or the point of one half may be brought to touch the base of the other. These all produce different shapes.

Turning a six-pointed star (centre of revolution through the valleys)

1 First make an accurate, dimensioned drawing of the six-pointed star. Prepare the blank from two pieces each 4in (100mm) long by 3⁵/₃₂in (80mm) wide by 1⁹/₁₆in (40mm) thick. Glue them together with a newspaper/glue joint so that the blank will now be 3⁵/₃₂in (80mm) square. Leave the glue to dry then turn to a cylinder, wasting as little diameter as possible. Here, I am using castello boxwood.

Hold the prepared blank in a chuck, supporting the tailstock end with a revolving cup centre, and turn to an accurate 2³/₄in (70mm) diameter. An end valley will be turned into the end face, so begin by turning the end face flat and true.

From the tailstock end measure and mark a series of lines in pencil. Line A will be the start point, the edge at the tailstock end. The next is set ²⁵/₃₂in (20mm) away from that tailstock edge, this is line B. From line B measure a further ³/₈in (10mm) and mark line C. From line C measure ³/₈in (10mm) and mark line D. From line D measure ²⁵/₃₂in (20mm) to locate line E. Withdraw the tailstock and mark, on the end face, a 1³/₈in (35mm) diameter, concentric pencil circle.

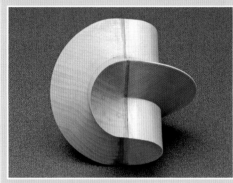

Twisted six-pointed star

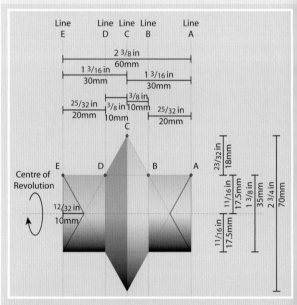

1 Six-pointed star, centre of revolution through the valleys

2 Draw a card template as before.

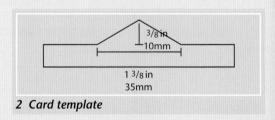

2 Card template

3

4

5

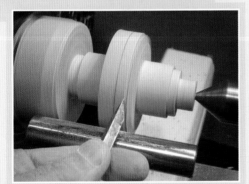

6

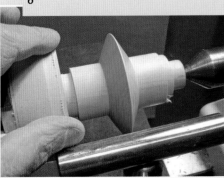

7

3 Use the card template to mark the white guideline on the specially ground slicing tool as before.

The slicing tool, pictured on page 84, is supported with a shelf toolrest whilst the end valley is being turned. Regularly check the shape of the end valley using the template. Make alterations to the angle of the cut where needed. When the template is a good fit, and the tool has cut to the correct depth, remove the toolrest then sand and polish the hollow. Fit a turned plug, with cloth buffer, into the turned valley and bring the tailstock up for support.

4 On the tailstock side of line B turn down to 1³/₈in (35mm) diameter.

5 On the headstock side of line D, and between lines D and E, turn down to 1³/₈in (35mm) diameter. On the headstock side of line E turn to about 1⁷/₃₂in (30mm) diameter. This will define that area.

6 Next turn from the top of line C, towards the tailstock, down to the base of line B. Complete the shaping of the middle spike by turning from the top of line C, towards the headstock, down to the base of line D.

7 When the centre section has been completed, sand and polish. Now the piece can be parted off on the headstock side of line E.

8 Now this is the nice bit. Use the wood remaining in the chuck to make a jam chuck. This will hold the work so that the second end valley can be turned.

9 Face off the wood in the chuck and turn a 1³/₈in (35mm) diameter 1⁹/₁₆in (40mm) deep hollow. Make sure that it is a tight fit for the turned end of the star blank. If the fit is slightly loose, press a sheet of newspaper around the blank and into the hollow to improve the grip.

10 Gently tap the work into place. When you are satisfied that the jam fit is tight and that the work is running on centre, the end face is turned flat and true. Do not remove too much wood. The end valley may now be turned using the slicing tool, as before.

11 Continue to check with the card template and make adjustments to the angle where needed. When satisfied, sand and polish the hollow.

12 Removing the now fully turned star from the jam chuck is easy. Loosen the metal chuck and take the jam chuck and work to a workbench. Find the newspaper/glue joint line in the jam chuck and, using a blunt dinner knife, split that joint. The jam chuck will split in half, leaving the turned six pointed star ready to be split. Use a craft knife to start the split on the six-pointed star, then once the gap has begun to open finish with a blunt dinner knife. This will wedge the joint apart.

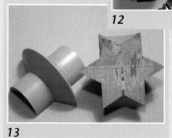

13 The picture shows the split six-pointed star. It can be twisted and rejoined to make an intriguing shape, or one half can be joined to the next six-pointed star (turned with the centre of revolution through the points) to make a hybrid shape, or it can be made into a twisted box. But to learn how to do that you will have to turn to Chapter 10.

Turning a Six-Pointed Star (centre of revolution through the points)

First make an accurate, dimensioned drawing of the six-pointed star with the centre of revolution through the points. Prepare the blank from two pieces each 4in (100mm) long by 2³/₄in (70mm) wide by 1³/₄in (35mm) thick. Glue them together with a newspaper/glue joint so that the blank will now be 2³/₄in (70mm) square. Leave the glue to dry then turn to a cylinder, wasting as little diameter as possible. Here I am using castello boxwood.

Hold the prepared blank in a chuck, supporting the tailstock end with a revolving cup centre, and turn to an accurate 2³/₈in (60mm) diameter. Measuring from the tailstock end towards the headstock, measure and mark pencil lines as follows: ³/₈in (9mm) for line A, followed by ¹¹/₁₆in (17.5mm) for line B, a further ¹¹/₁₆in (17.5mm) to locate line C, another ¹¹/₁₆in (17.5mm) to locate line D and finally, ¹¹/₁₆in (17.5mm) to position line E.

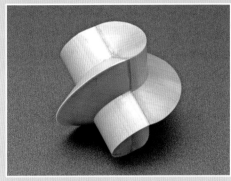

Twisted six-pointed star

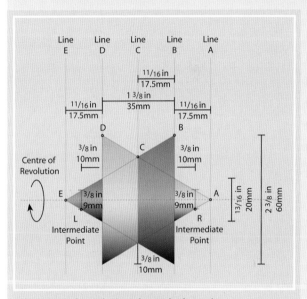

1 Centre of revolution through the points

Between lines A and B, turn down to an accurate ¹³/₁₆in (20mm) diameter. Carefully trim the tailstock side of line B, using the nose point of a skew, ensuring that the trimmed end is square to the top surface.

Next turn the area between lines D and E down to an accurate ¹³/₁₆in (20mm) diameter. Again trim the face edge of line D, using a skew, so that it is square to the top surface. It is necessary to trim both those faces because if the parting tool were used on this edge when bringing the area down to the required diameter it would tear out the endgrain face, leaving an unsightly rough edge.

Now to turn the side valley. The card template made for the end valley for the previous six-pointed star can be used again.

3 Card template

4 A second card template will also need to be made. This will allow the first half of the valley to be accurately turned. Using the nose of the skew, mark line C. Now take a slicing cut from the right into that cut line at C. The slice cut will stop at that marked position.

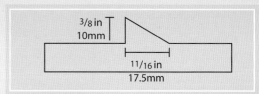

4 Card template

5 Continue to make those slicing cuts from the right and clean out the vee with vertical cuts from the skew on line C. Make regular checks with the half-template, making adjustments where necessary.

5

6 When the right hand half valley has been accurately turned the left hand half of the valley can be cut. This is much easier as the start and finish points can be clearly seen.

6

7 Test the card template in the side valley to make sure that the profile is correct. Make adjustments where necessary. The finished side valley can now be sanded and polished.

7

8 As before, when turning points, an intermediary position needs to be found part way along the turned tenon. This position, for the right hand point (R), is ³/₈in (10mm) away from the side face B towards the tailstock and for the left hand point (L), is ³/₈in (10mm) away from side face D towards the headstock. As it is difficult to fit a rule close to the tenon, a temporary mark is made on card and that is used to transfer the measurement to the tenon. At this position the tenon is turned down to ³/₈in (9mm) diameter on the headstock side of the marked line (L) and on the tailstock side of the line (R).

8

9 If the ¹³/₁₆ in (20mm) diameter position close to face B is joined to the new ³/₈in (9mm) diameter, with a sloping cut, the correct angle of the spike will have been produced. Repeat the process on the headstock side of the centrally turned side valley. Continue the sloping cuts on both sides but do not part off. Sand and polish both ends.

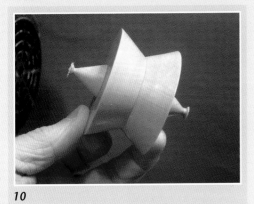

10 It is best to saw off on the waste side of the workpiece leaving small stubs on the ends. As the piece is turned from newspaper/glue joined wood fine diameters are far more vulnerable to twisting forces than solid wood. This could cause the tips to be twisted off.

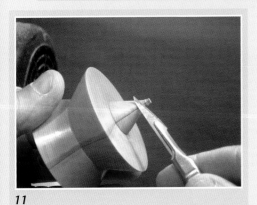

11 The points can be lightly trimmed to shape. Now the piece can be split apart using first a craft knife to carefully open the joint, and then a blunt dinner knife. The blunt dinner knife will wedge the joint open.

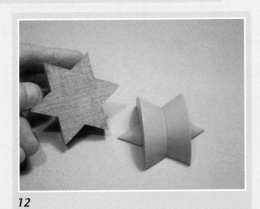

12 When split apart the six-pointed star profile is revealed. The split surfaces may be sanded and now choices have to be made. Do you glue the two halves together to make a wonderful twisted form? Do you take one half of this star with centre of rotation through the points and join it to one half of the star with centre of rotation through the valleys to make a hybrid shape? Or do you make it into a box (see Chapter 10) and mix the lids, sometimes hybrid, sometimes normal. Choices, choices, choices.

CHAPTER 9

BRANCH-SHAPED STREPTOHEDRONS

Having worked through the star-shaped forms I had to decide where the Weisflog cross shape fitted into the overall pattern. It was not part of the star family, nor was it one of the basic regular polygons. From this cross shape a whole new set of shapes developed with branches or arms (three, four, five and six) their ends square and the branch sides parallel. They produce, when split, twisted and rejoined, some of the most satisfying and complete shapes that I have so far produced.

The base shape has to have rotational symmetry so that when the piece has been fully turned, split, twisted and rejoined, a sinuous new form will be created. And as well as those immediate twisted shapes, hybrids can be created and boxes too. The turning and holding methods used to produce these branch shapes are exactly those used before to produce polygons and stars, end valleys, side valleys, dot-to-dot turnery and jam chucks with hot-melt glued supports.

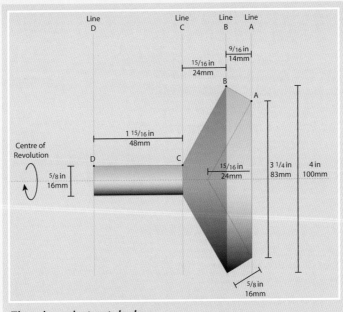

Three-branch streptohedron

Three-Branch Streptohedron

This three-branch shape is quite straightforward and easy to turn yet when the finished piece is split, twisted and rejoined, a most satisfying form is produced.

Twisted three-branch streptohedron

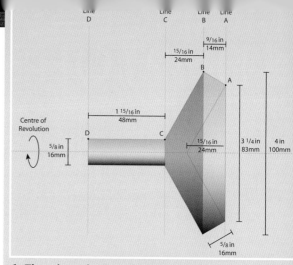

1 Three-branch streptohedron

1 Make an accurate, dimensioned drawing of the three-branch shape. Prepare the blank from two pieces each 5in (125mm) long by 4³⁄₈in (110mm) wide by 2³⁄₁₆in (55mm) thick. Glue them together with a newspaper/glue joint so that the blank is 4³⁄₈in (110mm) square. Leave to dry overnight then turn round to a cylinder wasting as little diameter as possible. Here I am using yew wood. Hold the prepared blank in a chuck, supporting the tailstock end with a cup centre, and turn to an accurate 4³⁄₁₆in (105mm) diameter.

2 Withdraw the tailstock and turn the end face flat and true.

3 From card, cut a template as shown.

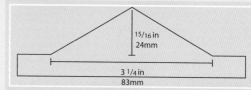

3 Template for end valley

4 Set the slicing tool, used previously to cut end valleys (see page 84), on the template and make a mark, using typists' correction fluid, lining up with the base line of the template. On the end face mark a 4in (100mm) diameter pencil circle as a guide. On the end face mark a second pencil circle 3¹⁄₄in (83mm) in diameter.

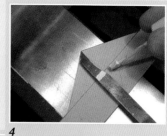

5 Use a shelf toolrest to support the specially ground slicing tool and begin turning in to produce the end valley, which has an outer diameter of 3¹⁄₄in (83mm). Use the template, and the white mark on the tool, to make sure that the end valley has the correct shape. Check the shape regularly, using the template, and make adjustments where necessary. When the template is a good fit the end valley can be sanded and polished.

6 Make a small turned plug to support the end of the work whilst turning the remaining parts. The plug will support the end of the work without creating splitting pressure. Place a small piece of cloth between the plug and the work to prevent marking the polished interior.

Now turn the blank to an accurate 4in (100mm) diameter. Mark, from the tailstock end of the blank (position A) towards the headstock, a series of pencil lines. From A measure and mark line B $9/16$in (14mm) away. From B, towards the headstock, measure and mark a further $15/16$in (24mm) to give line C. From line C, towards the headstock, measure and mark 1$15/16$in (48mm) to give line D.

7

8

7 The 3$1/4$in (83mm) diameter circle on the end face and line B are indicated here. These two points now have to be joined with a straight, clean cut (dot-to-dot turnery).

8 On the headstock side of line C, turn down to $5/8$in (16mm) diameter.

9

9 In the picture the positions B and C are indicated. When these are joined with a straight, clean cut, the correctly shaped angled face will have been produced. Now sand and polish the turned piece.

10

10 Re-mark the end of the $5/8$in (16mm) diameter branch to locate line D. Part off on the headstock side of line D. Here I am using a very narrow parting tool.

11

11 The completed piece.

12 Now split the turned part, and the Y-shape is revealed. Twist and glue the halves together to produce a sinuous form.

12

Four-Branch Streptohedron (centre of revolution through the flat sides)

This must be the easiest shape to turn. Just turn a cylinder then turn tenons at either end, part off and the job is done.

1 First make an accurate, dimensioned drawing of the cross-shaped piece. Prepare the blank from two pieces each 5in (125mm) long by 3in (76mm) wide by 1½in (38mm) thick. Glue them together with a newspaper/glue joint so that the blank will be 3in (76mm) square. Leave the glue to dry overnight. When satisfied that the glue is fully dry, turn to a cylinder. Turn the blank to an accurate 2¾in (68mm) diameter.

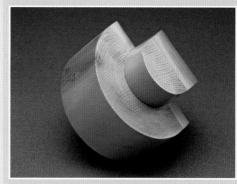

Twisted four branch streptohedron

Square off the end closest to the tailstock and, measuring from that edge, measure and mark with pencil lines the following distances: ⅜in (9mm) from the tailstock, (this will be a small area of waste wood), this pencil line will be line A. From line A, towards the headstock, measure ¹¹/₁₆in (17mm) marking line B. From line B, towards the headstock, measure 1⅜in (34mm) and mark line C. From line C measure ¹¹/₁₆in (17mm), towards the headstock, and mark line D.

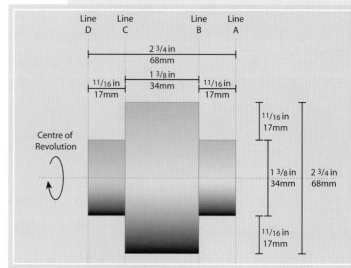

1 Four branch streptohedron

2 The waste area on the tailstock side of line A can now be turned down to 1⅜in (34mm) diameter. Use the waste section as a test area to turn to the required size. It is better to make mistakes on the waste wood. This will allow the area between lines A and B to be turned with more confidence.

Before the section between lines A and B is turned to exact size, use the corner of the parting tool to mark line A. This will leave a permanent mark showing the position from which to part off later. Turn close to line A but leave the pencil line intact so that the edge (which shows end grain) may be cleaned up later with a slicing cut from a skew chisel. Continue turning that section until it is an accurate 1⅜in (34mm) diameter.

2

3 Repeat the process at the headstock end, turning the waste wood to size close to the headstock, then, using the accurately turned waste wood as a guide, turn the section between lines C and D accurately to 1³⁄₈in (34mm) diameter. Again turn up to the pencil line of line C but leave intact so that the endgrain edge may be later trimmed with a slicing cut from a skew chisel.

4 The picture shows the nose of a skew chisel being used to slice the endgrain sides (lines B and D), leaving a good clean finish. Using a thin parting tool, begin to part off at line A (on the tailstock side) and line D (on the headstock side) but do not complete the parting off yet.

5 Sand and polish the turned piece, then complete the parting off, first at the tailstock, then at the headstock. When using these thin parting tools it will be noticed that the finish on the end grain is extremely good with very little tear-out. It is for this reason that I use them for the final parting cuts.

6 The finished piece may now be split and opened to reveal the cross, cross-section.

7 Twist one half against the other to create a twisted form or wait so that one half may be swapped with the shape turned on pages 108–11 to make a hybrid, or make this form into a twisted box as shown in Chapter 10.

Four-Branch Streptohedron (with centre of revolution through the valley)

Of all the finished shapes this one is the most difficult to decipher. When I show the finished piece and ask, 'What is its cross-section?' few are able to give the correct answer. It comes as a complete surprise when it is split and opened to reveal a basic cross.

Twisted four-branch streptohedron

1 Make an accurate, dimensioned drawing of the cross with the centre of revolution through the valleys. Prepare the blank from two pieces 5in (125mm) long by 3in (76mm) wide by 1¹/₂in (38mm) thick. Glue them together with a newspaper/glue joint so that the blank will now be 3in (76mm) square. Leave the blank to dry overnight. Set the blank between centres and round up to an accurate 2⁷/₈in (72mm) diameter. At the headstock end a small rebate is turned so that the piece may be held in a chuck. Once the piece is held in the chuck and is accurately recentred, the end face is turned flat and true. A ¹⁵/₁₆in (24mm) diameter pencil circle is marked on that end face.

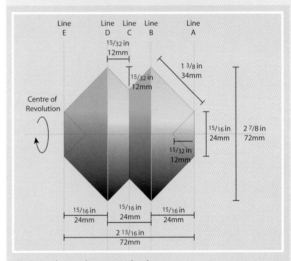

1 Four-branch streptohedron

2 From card make a template as shown. Set the slicing tool (see page 84) on the template so that the tip fits the end point. Make a mark, using typists' correction fluid, which lines up with its base line.

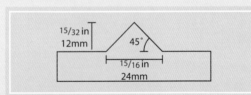

2 Template 1

3 Now, with a shelf toolrest supporting the slicing tool, cut in to form the valley in the end face. Make sure that the tool is cutting at centre height. Check with the template regularly, making sure that the angle is correct, make adjustments where necessary. When satisfied that the end valley is the correct shape and depth, sand and polish. Fit a turned plug into the end valley, with a small piece of cloth between it and the work to prevent marking, so that the centre may be brought up to support the work.

3

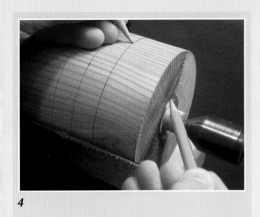

4

From the edge closest to the tailstock (line A) mark pencil lines, always towards the headstock, at the following positions. Measure from line A $^{15}/_{16}$in (24mm) to mark line B. From B measure $^{15}/_{32}$in (12mm) for line C. Measure another $^{15}/_{32}$in (12mm) from C to give line D. From line D measure a final $^{15}/_{16}$in (24mm) to locate line E.

4 If the rim of the end valley is joined to line B, with a clean straight cut, the first sloping side will have been produced.

5

5 Make sure that the side is flat and true. It will be noticed that a gouge is being used to cut this side. It is not always necessary to use a skew chisel. Take heart.

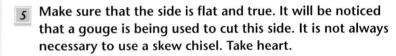

6 Template 2

6 Now for the side valley. To make this vee an easier cut it is created in two steps. The first is from line B down to meet line C at 1$^7/_8$in (48mm) diameter. It is difficult to measure accurately the diameter at the base of a vee cut so I use a simple card half vee template as a guide.

7 On line C, using the point of a skew chisel, make a light vertical cut. Now, from the right, slice down to meet that cut. Continue these cuts until a reasonable sized vee cut has been made.

6

8 This can be checked using the half vee template. The vee can be adjusted to match the template by making the slope more, or less, steep. Continue slicing, and checking until the vee cut conforms to the template.

8

9 The left hand half of the vee cut side valley is far simpler to produce. The start (line D) and finish (line C at the base of the vee) need to be joined with a clean, straight cut. The finished valley can be checked using the same template that was used to check the end valley. Next turn, on the headstock side of line E, down to $^{15}/_{16}$in (24mm) diameter.

9

10 The pencils indicate the 'dots' to be joined. Carefully turn this side to the correct angle using a gouge.

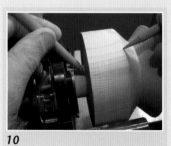

10

11 The almost complete shape.

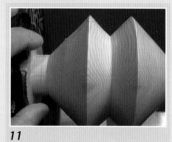

11

12 Sand and polish before parting off with a thin parting tool. The blank shape now needs to be held so that the final end valley may be turned. Cut an 8in (200mm) diameter, 2in (50mm) thick disc of softwood and fit it to a faceplate.

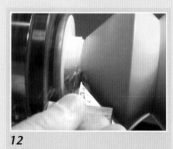

12

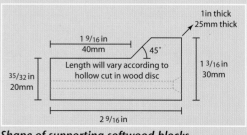

1 9/16 in
40mm

45°

1in thick
25mm thick

Length will vary according to
hollow cut in wood disc

1 3/16 in
30mm

35/32 in
20mm

2 9/16 in

Shape of supporting softwood blocks

13

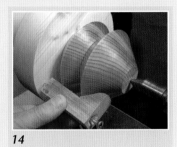

14

15

16

17

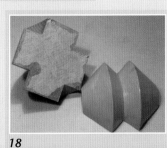

18

13 Into the face of that disc turn a sloping hollow into which the angled face of the blank will fit snugly.

14 Cut four softwood angle supports. The approximate dimensions for these are given in the illustration. Please note, the dimensions of these angled supports will vary according to the depth of the sloping hollow that is cut into the softwood disc.

15 Press the blank into the sloping hollow and screw the angle supports tightly down around the outer edge. As extra security, apply hot-melt glue between the supports and the angled face of the blank. The hot-melt glue will make a good temporary bond with the streptohedron blank but as the blank has a polished surface it will easily be removed without leaving any residue.

16 Bring the shelf toolrest across the face of the work. Rotate the lathe by hand to make sure that nothing catches, then switch on the lathe. The final end valley may be turned in exactly the same way as the first. Check the hollow using the template, making any adjustments necessary before sanding and polishing.

17 The completed four-branch streptohedron surrounded by the softwood supports. Note the clean polished surface. The hot-melt glue gripped the surface but left no marks.

18 Finally split the piece and open up to reveal the cross shape. Twist and rejoin to make an interesting shape. Mix one half of this with one half of the previous cross form to make a hybrid shape or they can be made into the most fascinating pair of boxes as described in Chapter 10.

Five-Branch Streptohedron

This piece is turned from olive wood, a most pleasant and easy working wood with an attractive grain and delicate oily scent. Its only drawback is that if it is not fully dry it can rapidly split, completely spoiling the work (don't use part seasoned stock).

Twisted five-branch

1. Make an accurate, dimensioned drawing of the five-branch piece (see Chapter 3). Prepare the blank from two pieces each 5⁹/₁₆in (140mm) long by 4in (100mm) wide by 2in (50mm) thick. Glue them together with a newspaper/glue joint so that the blank is 4in (100mm) square. Leave the blank to dry overnight then turn to a cylinder, wasting as little diameter as possible. Hold the prepared blank in a chuck, supporting the tailstock end with a revolving cup centre. Now turn to an accurate 3⁹/₁₆in (90mm) diameter.

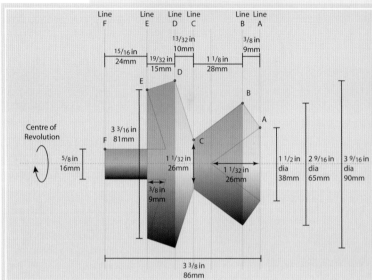

1 Five-branch streptohedron

2. Cut a card template as shown. The diameter and depth are shown to provide the correct shape for the end valley.

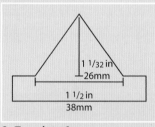

2 Template 1

3. Set the specially ground slicing tool (see page 84) on the template, aligning the points and mark, using typists' correction fluid, the position of the base line. Withdraw the tailstock and turn the end face flat and true. Upon that end face mark a 1¹/₂in (38mm) diameter pencil circle.

3

4. With the slicing tool, set on a shelf toolrest and the white mark on the tool set parallel to the end face, begin to slice into that end face to create the valley. Make sure that the tool is cutting at centre height. Make regular checks with the template to ensure that the angle of the valley is correct. Make adjustments where necessary. Sand and polish the end valley.

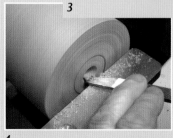

4

Bring the tailstock back to support the work, fitting a turned plug between the centre and the wood. Starting at the tailstock end of the work and moving towards the headstock, mark a series of pencil lines. The edge of the end face will be line A. From line A measure 3/8in (9mm) to mark line B. From line B measure 1 1/8in (28mm) for line C. From line C measure 13/32in (10mm) for line D. From line D measure 19/32in (15mm) to position line E. And finally, from E measure 15/16in (24mm) to mark line F.

5

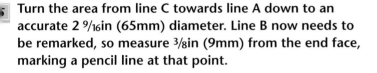

Turn the area from line C towards line A down to an accurate 2 9/16in (65mm) diameter. Line B now needs to be remarked, so measure 3/8in (9mm) from the end face, marking a pencil line at that point.

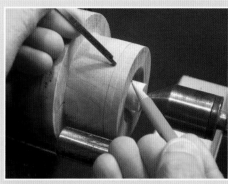

6

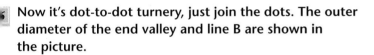

Now it's dot-to-dot turnery, just join the dots. The outer diameter of the end valley and line B are shown in the picture.

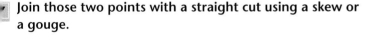

Join those two points with a straight cut using a skew or a gouge.

7

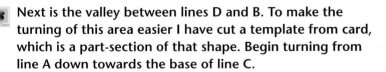

Next is the valley between lines D and B. To make the turning of this area easier I have cut a template from card, which is a part-section of that shape. Begin turning from line A down towards the base of line C.

35/32 in
20mm

1 1/8 in
28mm

90°

8 Template 2

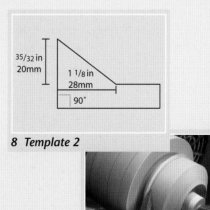

8

9 Check the angle of the sloping cut with the template and make adjustments to that cut as necessary.

9

10 This next cut is much easier because the start and finish points can clearly be seen. So join line D with the base of line C.

10

11 Use a skew or a gouge to cut this angled edge. A skew will be needed to clean up the vee cut in the base of this valley.

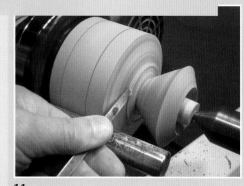

11

12 On the headstock side of line E, turn down to ⁵⁄₈in (16mm) diameter.

12

13 On the inside face of line E mark, from the top edge down, ¹¹⁄₆₄in (4.5mm). Join the top edge of line D with the newly marked pencil line on the inner face of E to produce the sloping edge of DE.

13

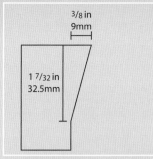

3/8 in
9mm

1 7/32 in
32.5mm

14 Template 3

15

16

17

18

14 From card make a third template as shown in the illustration. This will help the shaping of the undercut behind face E.

15 Set the shelf toolrest as close to face E as possible. Set the slicing tool on that toolrest and position it so that it will cut at the correct angle.

16 Begin to make the cuts.

17 Check regularly with the template. Make adjustments to the angle where needed. When satisfied that the shape is good, the whole piece may be sanded and polished. The end position, F, may need to be re-marked. Always be generous, for wood may be cut off but not reapplied. Part off on the headstock side of line F using a thin parting tool.

18 Carefully split the finished piece then open to reveal the five-branch shape. This is a most satisfying shape. Take the two halves, twist and join them and two different forms will be discovered. Move the edge of one half to the side of the other half to produce one form or the edge of one half to the base of the other to produce a second form. And, of course, they can also be right or left handed.

Six-Branched Streptohedron (centre of rotation through the valleys)

This first form is relatively easy to turn but to make it easier still I have chosen to turn it from sapele. Most of the turning is between centres. A simple jam chuck is used to complete the turning.

Twisted six branch

1 Make an accurate, dimensioned drawing of the six branch shape. Prepare the blank from two pieces each 5³/₁₆in (130mm) long by 4in (100mm) wide by 2in (50mm) thick. Glue them together with a newspaper/glue joint so that the blank will now be 4in (100mm) square. Leave the glue to dry overnight then turn the blank to a cylinder, wasting as little diameter as possible.

Hold the prepared blank in a chuck, supporting the tailstock end with a revolving cup centre. Withdraw the tailstock and turn the end face flat and true. On that end face mark a 1¹/₁₆in (27mm) diameter pencil circle.

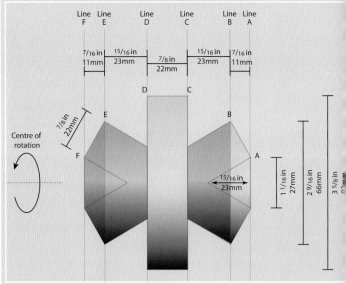

1 Six-branch streptohedron

2 From card, cut a template that will act as a guide to the internal shape of the end valley.

3 Take the specially shaped slicing tool (see page 84) and set it on the template so that their points are aligned. The position of the base line is marked on the slicing tool using typists' correction fluid.

Bring the shelf toolrest across the face of the work with the slicing tool in place and set so that it will cut at centre height. Make sure that the white mark on the slicing tool is set parallel to the end face then begin to slice into the work. Check regularly with the template, making adjustments to the angled face where necessary.

When satisfied that the end valley is correct, sand and polish. Into that end valley fit a turned plug and bring the centre up to support the work. Turn the piece to an accurate 3⁵/₈in (92mm) diameter.

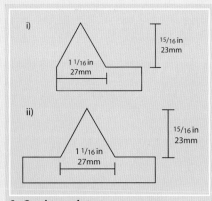

2 Card templates

3

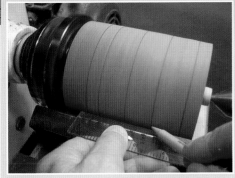

5 Mark a series of pencil lines upon the turned blank, working from the tailstock end, which will be line A, towards the headstock. So from line A measure $^7/_{16}$in (11mm) for line B, from B measure $^{15}/_{16}$in (23mm) for line C, from C measure $^7/_8$in (22mm) for line D, from D measure $^{15}/_{16}$in (23mm) for line E and from line E measure $^7/_{16}$in (11mm) for line F.

6 On the tailstock side of line C turn down to an accurate $2^9/_{16}$in (66mm) diameter.

7 Having turned away some wood, line B needs to be re-marked, so measure $^7/_{16}$in (11mm) from the face end and mark a pencil line. Join that point to the $1^1/_{16}$in (27mm) diameter opening of the end valley, making sure that the angled face is flat and true.

8 Now to turn the side valley between lines B and C. Slice down from the right into the area between B and C. Trim vertically down line C to clean up the cut.

9 Use the card template (i) – this is the same template that was used for the end valley – to check that the angle is correct and make adjustments where needed. A thin parting tool can be used to slice vertically down line C as this tool will leave the endgrain edge cleanly cut.

10 Use a thin parting tool to slice vertically down, on the headstock side, of line D. The white mark that can be seen on the tool is a depth guide.

10

11 On the headstock side of line F turn to an accurate 1$\frac{1}{16}$in (27mm) diameter. Next turn the area between line E and D down to 2$\frac{9}{16}$in (66mm) diameter.

11

12 Line E needs to be marked again, so measure from the edge of line F, $\frac{7}{16}$in (11mm) towards the headstock.

12

13 The angled face between E and D now needs to be cut, so slice down from E towards D. Regularly check the angle using template (i) on page 116.

13

14 Make adjustments to the angle of the cut as necessary.

14

15 Continue to slice down joining line E to D but an adapted template will need to be used to check the valley angle as it becomes deeper. For template sizes see the illustration on page 116.

15

16

16 Now join line E to the 1¹/₁₆in (27mm) diameter end of line F. Sand and polish the part-turned piece.

17 Carefully part off on the headstock side of line F. The picture shows the almost completed piece.

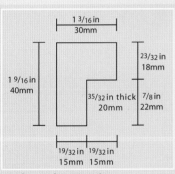

17

18

18 To turn the final end valley the work will be held in a jam chuck made from 2in (50mm) thick softwood. So cut a 12in (300mm) diameter softwood disc and mount it on a faceplate. Turn the edge and face flat and true. In the centre of the softwood disc turn a 2³/₈in (66mm) diameter hole 1³/₄in (45mm) deep to accept the valley turned end of the piece. Push the piece into the hollow, making sure that it sits evenly with face C resting on the softwood surface.

```
          1 3/16 in
           30mm
    ┌─────────────────┐
                           23/32 in
                            18mm
1 9/16 in
 40mm           35/32 in thick   7/8 in
                  20mm          22mm

      19/32 in  19/32 in
       15mm     15mm
```

Softwood supporting block sizes

19 Cut four L-shaped supports from softwood. See the illustration for the dimensions. These are screwed around the edge of the turned piece and pressed well against its sides adding support. Small tacks of hot-melt glue between the supports and the workpiece provide additional grip. Bring the shelf toolrest across the face of the work and rotate the chuck by hand to make sure nothing catches before switching the lathe on. The end valley may now be turned in exactly the same manner as shown previously. Sand and polish the end valley.

19

20

20 Remove the finished piece from the jam chuck and carefully split the newspaper/glue joint to reveal the six-branch shape. The piece may be twisted and rejoined or a hybrid can be formed once the next six-legged shape has been turned.

Six-Branch Streptohedron (centre of rotation through the branch)

1 Make an accurate, dimensioned drawing of the six-branch shape. Prepare the blank from two pieces each 5 3/16in (130mm) long by 4in (100mm) wide by 2in (50mm) thick. Glue them together with a newspaper/glue joint so that the blank will now be 4in (100mm) square. Leave the glue to dry overnight then turn the blank round, wasting as little diameter as possible. Hold the prepared blank in a chuck supporting the tailstock end with a revolving cup centre. Turn to an accurate 3 17/32in (90mm) diameter.

Working from the tailstock end towards the headstock measure and mark pencil lines at the following distances. 3/8in (9mm) from the edge will position line A. From line A measure 9/16in (14mm) to position line B. From line B 3/4in (18.5mm) gives line C. A further 9/16in (13 1/2mm) will provide the centre line, line D. From line D measure 9/16in (13.5mm) for line E. From line E 3/4in (18.5mm) gives line F. And finally 14mm (9/16in) from F positions line G.

Twisted six branch

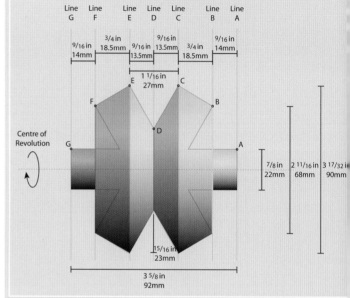

1 Six branch streptohedron

2 Begin by turning the side valley between lines C and E. A simple card template is made to help this process.

2 Card template (i)

3 Make a vertical slicing cut with the tip of the skew on line D, then a slicing cut from right to left. Check with template number (i) adjusting and cutting until half the side valley, from C to D, is accurately cut.

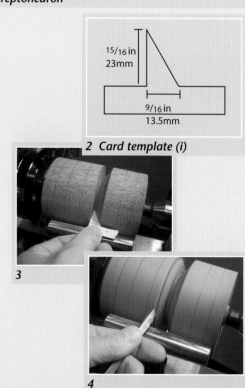

4 Now join the top of line E to the base of the valley.

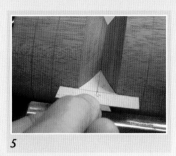

5 Check the shape of the valley using the template from page 116. Next turn, on the tailstock side of line B, down to $2^{11}/_{16}$ in (68mm) diameter. On the headstock side of line F, turn down to $2^{11}/_{16}$in (68mm) diameter.

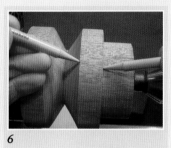

6 Now join the dots.

7 Join line C to the base of line B, with a straight clean cut.

8 Next, on the left hand end, join line E to the base of line F with a straight, clean cut.

9 Begin turning on the tailstock side of line B down to $^{7}/_{8}$in (22mm) diameter.

10 On the headstock side of line F, turn down to $^{7}/_{8}$in (22mm) diameter.

11 From a cheap wood chisel or a piece of high carbon steel grind the shape shown opposite.

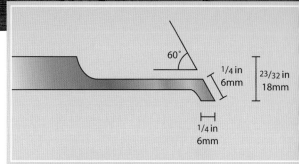

11 *Plan view of ground slicing tool 6mm thick*

12 Both ¼in (6mm) wide faces are ground back at 40° on the underside to produce a cutting edge.

13 Use the shelf toolrest to support the tool, which will be cutting at centre height, and gently slice in behind line F.

14 From card, cut template number (ii). Use this template to check the undercut valley.

Template (ii)

15 Next turn the undercut valley at the tailstock end. Bring the shelf toolrest to support the slicing tool, cutting at centre height, and cut in under line B.

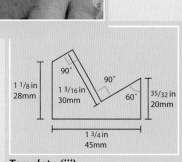

Template (iii)

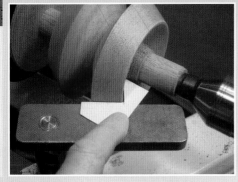

16

16 Cut card template number (iii) as shown. This can be used to check the accuracy of the undercut valley.

17

17 Use the specially ground tool, shown earlier, to cut the ⁷⁄₈in (22mm) diameter arm cleanly.

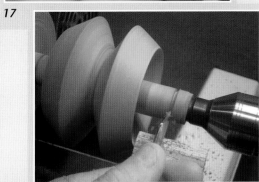

18

18 Lightly cut into lines A and G, but be generous and cut on the waste side of those lines for they can always be cut shorter but wood can never be added on. Sand and polish, then carefully part off at either end using a thin parting tool.

19

19 The finished piece is ready to be split...

20

21

20 ...to reveal the six-branched interior. Now twist and rejoin to see the shape produced or, better still, take one half of the six-branch turned through the valleys and join with one half turned through the 'legs' to make a hybrid shape. Interestingly the hybrid has two forms, one twists from top to bottom, the other consists of two curved flats, one of which is a continuous ribbon, while the other has a stop at either end.

21 So far all these shapes have been turned with straight sides and edges. Why not try some with curves? There are many undiscovered shapes to try. If you are more adventurous, work out how these were turned and turn some for yourself.

Peter Rand, having produced numerous femispheres, decided that the finished work would look much better if the glue joints between the two halves were either celebrated by either accenting them, or removed, and these effects can be seen in some of his more sculptural examples. In addition he realized that the intrigue and fascination of these objects would be increased if, when completed, the grain pattern matched all round.

Here is how Peter arranges the blank so that this can be done:

Baltic birch femisphere by Peter Rand

1 Cut a crude, large enough blank where the hedron cross-section of the strepthedron will be. Use as narrow a kerf as possible and cut as flat as possible – (sand perfectly plane if necessary).

2 Identify two central points, one on each cut face, which are from identical points within the grain pattern. This is easily done since the complex grain pattern on the cut faces will exactly match, provided the kerf was narrow enough.

3 Use these two points as a pivot around which the two halves will be rotated **before** turning the streptohedron shape. A pin can be conveniently inserted to make the two points an actual pivot and to help hold the pieces together.

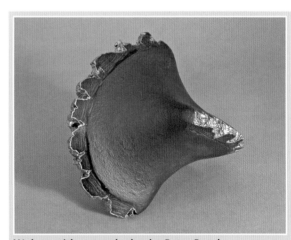

Walnut with natural edge by Peter Rand

4 Assemble the pieces on their pivot and align the grain exactly as it is naturally.

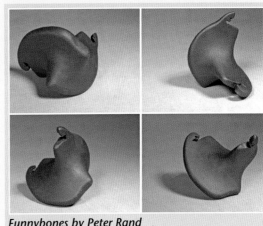

Funnybones by Peter Rand

5 Rotate the pieces from that natural position by the exact angle of the hedron required (90° for a sphericon, etc) and fix in place. Peter uses cable ties but a newspaper/glue joint is a safer option.

6 Turn the streptohedron shape. It must be turned exactly through the pivot point, and the edges carefully related to it. Hose clamps of various sizes can be shifted along the turning as it progresses. These also allow the two halves to be reversibly rotated to the natural position as the turning progresses to check the matching both of the edges and of the grain.

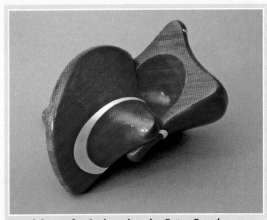

Purpleheart femisphere box by Peter Rand

7 Split the finished piece and rotate back to the original orientation to form the streptohedron. The grain **must** match. Small mismatches can usually be corrected by sanding the assembly in the original orientation.

Peter uses graph paper on the cut faces to determine and mark centres, angles, turning axes, etc. With such tricks and a bit of sanding after turning, he can get the grain to match within the error created by the kerf of the original cut. That error, he says, depends on the fineness and orientation of the grain, but is usually small – fractions of a millimetre.

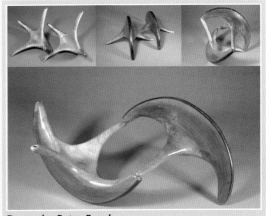

Dance by Peter Rand

CHAPTER 10

BOXES
WITH A TWIST

Here I will describe two methods used to make boxes from these streptohedron shapes. The first method explains how boxes are made from streptohedrons by turning matching hollows into their split faces. This will allow the lid to be twisted on the base to make the streptohedron form and back to make the basic form. It will also allow hybrid boxes to be made where a lid from one streptohedron can be mixed with the base from another, producing unusual twists and turns.

In the second method, the interior hollow is turned in the blank first. The outer shape is then turned to reflect its interior.

The first box making method shows how the streptohedron halves may be held, first an epoxy car-body filler (Bondo) chuck and second, in a polyurethane foam chuck. This will enable accurate hollows to be turned into their split faces whilst each half is firmly held. See Chapter 2 for a description of how these chucks are made. In these examples I will use prepared pieces so that the lids of each box will mix and match with the base of the other to make hybrid shapes. The method of producing the streptohedrons used for the first box-making procedure is described in Chapter 9. They are of the same size as described there.

Boxes with a twist

IMPORTANT NOTE

If these boxes are to be turned using imperial measurements it is best to prepare accurate drawings using imperial measurements before beginning to turn.

Four-Branch Streptohedron Box (rotated through the valleys)

Turn the cross-shaped streptohedron as described in Chapter 9 using the dimensions as shown in the illustration on page 108. Make a car body filler chuck to fit the streptohedron, which has been turned, as described in Chapter 2, page 20. For the sleeve, which is fitted into the turned face of the streptohedron half, prepare a small wood cylinder which is 1¼in (32mm) diameter and ¹¹⁄₁₆in (18mm) long.

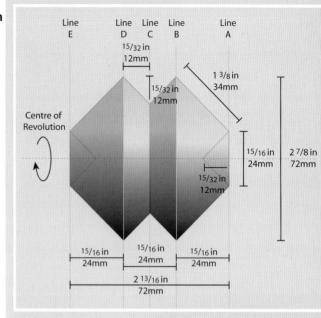

Cross section

1 Hold the first streptohedron half in the prepared car body filler chuck. Screw the collar down to hold the work firmly.

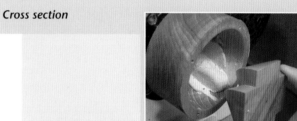

2 Mark a 1¼in (32mm) diameter pencil circle (the diameter of the prepared wood cylinder) on the face of the half held in the wood chuck.

3 Using a small square-end tool supported on a shelf toolrest, turn on the inside of that marked line to a depth of ⅝in (15mm).

4

4 Using white PVA glue, fit the prepared plug into the turned hollow. Use the tailstock to press it home. Allow the glue to dry.

5

5 Turn into the plug to a depth of $^{11}/_{16}$in (18mm), leaving a wall thickness of $^{1}/_{8}$in (3mm). Sand and polish the turned hollow.

6

6 Remove the chuck collar and take out the finished half. Fit the second half into the chuck. Set a pair of callipers to $1^{1}/_{4}$in (32mm) diameter (the size of the turned cylindrical plug) and mark a pencil circle of that diameter on the face of the half now held in the wood chuck.

7 On the inside of the marked pencil circle, turn to a depth of $^{5}/_{8}$in (15mm). A square-end tool supported on a shelf toolrest is used to turn the hollow into the face of the work. Sand and polish the interior of the hollow.

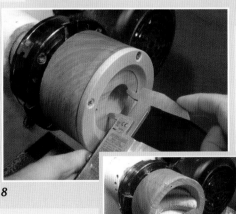

8

8 Using callipers, still set to $1^{1}/_{4}$in (32mm), check the size of the opening before removing the work from the chuck.

9 Fit the two halves together to make the first of the streptohedron boxes. Twist the top to alter its shape.

9

Four-Branch Streptohedron box (rotated through the flats)

These halves will be held in polyurethane foam chuck. Turn the cross-shaped streptohedron as described on page 106 using the dimensions shown. The polyurethane foam chuck to hold these streptohedron halves is produced as described in Chapter 2.

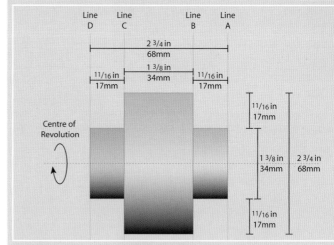

Four-branch streptohedron with centre of revolution through the arms

1   Prepare a small turned cylinder which is 1¼in (32mm) diameter and ¹¹/₁₆in (18mm) long. Fit the first streptohedron half into the foam chuck.

2   Screw the collar down to hold it firmly.

3   Set a pair of callipers to 1¼in (32mm) diameter (the size of the turned cylindrical plug) and mark that size on the face of the half held in the wood chuck.

4   Using a small square-ended tool, supported on a shelf toolrest, turn on the inside of that marked line to a depth of ⅝in (15mm).

5   Using white PVA glue, fit the plug into the turned hollow. Allow the glue to dry.

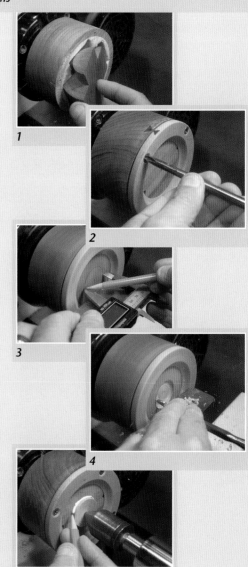

6

6 Turn into the glued plug to a depth of 18mm (¹¹/₁₆in), leaving a wall thickness of about 3mm (¹/₈in). When satisfied, sand and polish.

7

7 Remove the collar and the finished half.

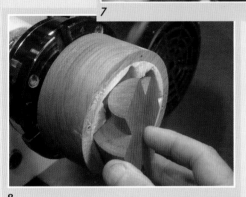

8

8 Fit the remaining half into the foam hollow. It will fit perfectly. Set a pair of callipers to 1¹/₄in (32mm) diameter (the size of the turned cylindrical plug) and mark that size on the face of the half held in the wood chuck.

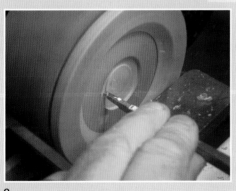

9

9 Using a small square-ended tool supported on a shelf toolrest turn on the inside of that marked line to a depth of ⁵/₈in (15mm).

10 It is best to check the diameters of each of the inserts, to make sure that they will fit both hollows before removing the last piece.

10

11 Remove the piece from the chuck and fit it to the matching half to make the box. Twist the top to alter its shape.

11

A pair of boxes have now been made and, because their cross-sections are the same, they will have interchangeable lids. Just mix, match and twist.

1

1 This picture shows the parts and the chucks.

2

2

2 These pictures show the boxes with their lids, straight from the lathe.

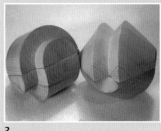

3

3 Next the lids are twisted.

4

4 And finally the lids are exchanged to make hybrids. Buff up on a polishing mop to remove any superficial blemishes.

5

5 Any of the streptohedron forms can be made into boxes using the techniques described above. When making chucks to hold those halves it is not always necessary to infill the hemispherical hollows with epoxy resin or polyurethane foam but generally it helps support the shape and prevents damage to their surface whilst they are being turned. The lids may be held in place using small rare earth magnets to act as closures.

A Hexagonal Box with a Matching Internal Hexagonal Hollow

The blank is prepared with an internal hollow before the outer profile is turned. Prepare a blank from two pieces of hardwood, here I have used English yew, each 5³/₁₆in (130mm) long by 3⁵/₃₂in (80mm) wide by 1⁹/₁₆in (40mm) thick. Plane one face of each flat and true. Glue those faces together, with newspaper between, to produce a finished blank 3⁵/₃₂in (80mm) square.

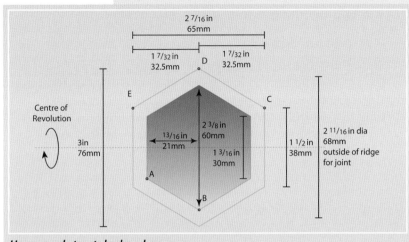

Hexagonal streptohedron box

1. Set between centres (use a cup centre at the tailstock) and turn almost round, leaving a small flat on one, or more, sides. Turn a step at both ends to fit the chuck that will be used to hold the piece. From the edge at the tailstock end, measure ¹⁹/₁₆in (40mm) and mark a pencil line. Mark a pencil datum across that line so that the pieces, when reassembled, will have matching grain.

2. Remove the blank from the lathe and take it to the bandsaw. Lay the flat edge on the table and cut, straight and square, through the marked line. The flat edge provides a firm base when cutting.

3. Hold the shorter section in a chuck. Make sure that it runs on centre then turn the face flat and true. A ridge will be turned upon the face of this half-blank and a matching groove turned in the opposite half of the blank so that they can be accurately fitted back together.

4. On the face of the work mark a 2¹¹/₁₆in (68mm) diameter pencil circle. On the outside of that line turn a ¹/₁₆in (1.5mm) deep step flat and true. Next measure ¹/₁₆in (1.5mm) away from the inside of the marked line and turn, towards the centre, a ¹/₁₆in (1.5mm) deep step, again flat and true. This will leave a small raised ridge ¹/₁₆in (1.5mm) high and wide. The internal hollow may now be turned.

5 On the face of the revolving work mark two concentric pencil circles, the first 1³/₁₆in (30mm) diameter, the second 2³/₈in (60mm) diameter. Take a ¹/₈in (3mm) wide square-end tool and make a white depth mark ¹³/₁₆in (21mm) from its tip.

Set a shelf toolrest in the toolpost to firmly support the square-end tool so that it cuts at centre height. Use the square-end tool to turn out the 1³/₁₆in (30mm) diameter hole to ¹³/₁₆in (21mm) deep. A drill may be used instead but it must stop short of the full depth so that the hold made by the centre spur may be turned away.

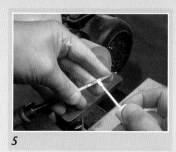

5

6

6 To create the correct angle for the internal hollow in this half...

7

7 ...just join the base edge of the hole with the marked 2³/₈in (60mm) pencil circle.

8 Make sure that the sloping side is flat. Carefully sand and polish but do not round over the top edge for this is part of the joint line. Remove this half from the chuck and set it to one side. Mount the second half of the blank in the chuck, making sure that it runs on centre. Turn the face flat and true.

8

9 Measure the diameter of the turned, raised ridge from the first half. This precise measurement must be used to mark a pencil circle on the face of the second half.

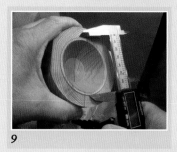

9

10 This measured diameter is the diameter that must actually be turned. (You may have turned slightly larger or smaller than the dimension provided.)

10

11 On the inside of this pencil circle, turn a $^1/_{16}$in (1.5mm) deep by $^1/_{16}$in (1.5mm) wide groove.

11

12 Test the two parts together and make alterations until the fit is exact. Mark two concentric pencil circles at 1$^1/_{16}$in (30mm) and 2$^3/_8$in (60mm) diameters on the face of the blank.

12

13 Now it is a repeat of the first half. Turn the centre hole $^{13}/_{16}$in (21mm) deep, join the base of this hole to the marked 2$^3/_8$in (60mm) pencil circle then sand and polish.

13

14 The two halves are now ready to join. Test them for fit, aligning the pencil datum mark. As end grain will be joined to end grain, apply polyurethane glue to both edges for an extra-strong bond.

14

15 Refit the glued halves, re-aligning the pencil datum mark, compressing the glued blank between cup centre and chuck until the glue has set. The re-aligning joint and the pencil datum marks will ensure that inside and outside line up and that the newspaper/glue joint is in line and able to be split later.

Turn the blank to an accurate 3in (76mm) diameter. Measure 1$^7/_{32}$in (32.5mm) either side of the glue joint line and mark pencil lines. The glue joint corresponds to line D in the drawing, and the pencil lines to lines C and E. The outside of this hexagonal box may now be turned in exactly the same manner as described in Chapter 7.

15

16 On the tailstock side of the marked pencil line C, turn down to an accurate 1½in (38mm) diameter. Join the top of the joint line D to the start of the turned spigot with a straight cut. Repeat on the headstock side of the joint line to produce the outer profile of the box.

16

17 Sand and polish. Use a thin parting tool (as this cuts end grain cleanly) to part off at either end.

17

18 Then sand and polish the end grain.

18

19 Split the newspaper/glue joint to reveal the internal shaping.

19

20 Once the joint line on both halves has been sanded, cleaned and polished, small rare earth magnets can be fixed in the rims to act as closures. With thought and careful turning, any of these streptohedron shapes may be turned with matching hollow interiors.

20

An Art Deco Stepped Box

This shape has been turned from a piece of boxelder (Manitoba maple, *Acer negundo*) with a wonderful burl. The light burl sits well with the Art Deco style. Prepare a blank from two pieces of hardwood, each 6³/₈in (160mm) long by 3⁹/₁₆in (90mm) wide by 1³/₄in (45mm) thick. Plane one face of each flat and true. Glue these two faces together, with newspaper between, to produce a finished blank 3⁹/₁₆in (90mm) square.

Set between centres (use a cup centre at the tailstock) and turn almost round, leaving a small flat on one or more sides. Turn a step at both ends to fit the chuck that will be used to hold the piece.

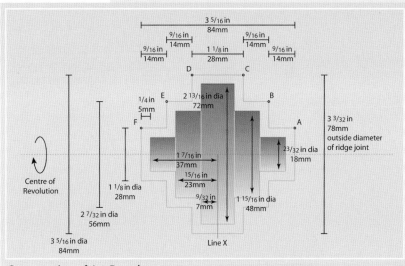

Cross-section of Art Deco box

1. Mark a pencil datum line along the length of the blank. From the tailstock end measure 2³/₁₆in (55mm) and mark a pencil line at that point. Take the blank from the lathe to a bandsaw and, with the flat side on the table, cut square and true through the marked line.

2. Fit the tailstock end into a chuck and centre accurately. Turn the end face flat and true. A ridge will be turned on the first half-blank and a matching groove turned into the second half-blank so that they can easily be fitted back together.

3. On the end face mark a 3³/₃₂in (78mm) diameter pencil circle for the ridge. Turn a step on the outside of that marked line ¹/₁₆in (1.5mm) deep. On the inside of the marked pencil circle turn ¹/₁₆in (1.5mm) away, turn a ¹/₁₆in (1.5mm) deep step towards the centre. This will leave a thin ridge.

4. Mark three concentric pencil circles, ²³/₃₂in (18mm), 1¹⁵/₁₆in (48mm) and 2¹³/₁₆in (72mm) diameters on the face of the work.

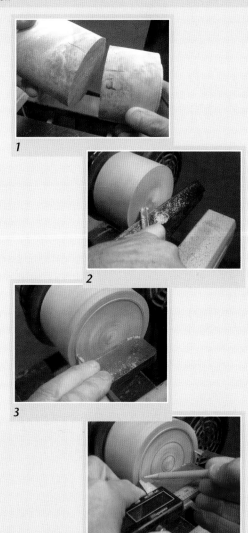

5 On a square-end tool make a white mark 1⁷/₁₆in (37mm) from the cutting edge. This will act as a depth guide. Fit a shelf toolrest into the toolpost to support the square-end tool so that it will cut at centre height.

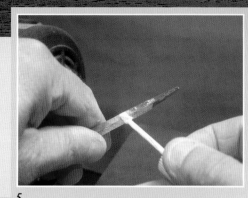

5

6 Turn out the ²³/₃₂in (18mm) diameter hole until the depth mark on the square-end tool is reached. The tool, when making the final cuts at the base of the hole, must be drawn lightly, and square, across the toolrest so that a fine cut is made. Keep the tool sharp to maintain a fine cut.

Make a white mark ¹⁵/₁₆in (23mm) from the edge of the square-end tool. On the inside of the 1¹⁵/₁₆in (48mm) pencil circle turn down to the marked depth on the tool. Make sure that the final cuts are light and crisp.

6

7 Make a white depth mark on the square-end tool ⁹/₃₂in (7mm) from the cutting edge. On the inside of the 2¹³/₁₆in (72mm) diameter pencil circle turn down to the depth mark.

7

8 Sand and polish the inside hollow, taking care not to round over the top edge which forms the joint line.

Remove the piece from the lathe and replace it with the second half. Centre the work accurately, this is important. If the blank is off-centre, lightly touch a pencil against the rotating piece. The pencil line will indicate the high side. Loosen the chuck very slightly and tap the pencil mark. This should bring it onto centre. If not, continue in this manner until the work is accurately centred, then tighten the chuck.

8

9 Turn the end face flat and true. Measure the thin ridge on the face of the first half. Use the callipers to mark this measured diameter on the face of the second piece. On the inside of this marked line turn a ¹/₁₆in (1.5mm) wide by ¹/₁₆in (1.5mm) deep groove.

9

10

10 Check that the groove fits the ridge, adjusting until the fit is exact.

11

11 Mark three concentric pencil circles on the face of the work, $^{22}/_{32}$in (18mm), $1^{15}/_{16}$in (48mm) and $2^{13}/_{16}$in (72mm). Turn them out and polish as before.

12 Now that the internal shaping is finished, the two halves may be glued together. Apply polyurethane glue to the turned faces, pressing the joint together.

12

13 Make sure that the datum line and the newspaper/glue joint are accurately lined up. Apply pressure from the tailstock whilst the glue sets.

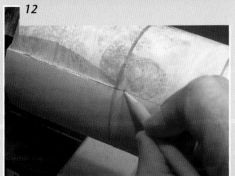

13

14 Allow the glue to set, then turn to an accurate $3^5/_{16}$in (84mm) outer diameter. From the centre-joint line (line X) measure, towards the tailstock, $^9/_{16}$in (14mm) to locate line C, then from C a further $^9/_{16}$in (14mm) to locate line B, then from B a further $^9/_{16}$in (14mm) to locate line A. Mark with pencil lines. From the centre-joint line (line X) measure, towards the headstock, $^9/_{16}$in (14mm) to locate line D, then from D a further $^9/_{16}$in (14mm) to locate line E and from E a further $^9/_{16}$in (14mm) to locate line F. Mark with pencil lines.

14

15 Using a thin parting tool, for this will cut end grain more cleanly, cut on the tailstock side of lines C and B. Mark on the parting tool a white depth mark for each line to help judge how deep to cut. $^9/_{16}$in (14mm) deep for line C and $1^1/_8$ (28mm) deep for line B.

Allow an extra $^1/_4$in (6mm) on the tailstock side of line A when cutting in with the parting tool. This will give a little leeway (extra length) which can be trimmed off later. This is just a cut to indicate the general position of line A.

15

16 Next, still using a thin parting tool, cut on the headstock side of lines D and E in the same way and to the depths indicated before. When cutting around line F, again allow an extra 1/4in (6mm), but on the headstock side this time, to give a little leeway. This cut is just to indicate the general position of line F.

16

17 Turn down the areas between those cut lines, to the required depths, using a wider parting tool. Make sure that the tool is kept sharp. It may be used like a mini skew chisel, cutting the wood to create a good finish. The areas between lines C and B and lines D and E are turned to an exact 2³/₁₆in (56mm) diameter.

17

18 The area between lines B and A and E and F, (plus that extra 1/4in (6mm) for leeway), are turned to an accurate 1¹/₈in (28mm) diameter.

18

19 At this point I noticed that the newspaper/glue joint was beginning to open. The box is quite thin and the newspaper/glue joint was beginning to give way. This does not often happen, but if it does here is what to do so that turning can safely continue. Secure a cable tie around the part of the work which is opening and continue carefully.

19

20 Sand and polish the top and the side that does not have the cable tie securing the parts.

20

21 Secure a cable tie around the completed part. Remove the cable tie from the area to be worked next. Sand and polish. When satisfied, refix a cable tie over the polished area. The work may now be parted off. Here I have used a temporary toolrest, made from wood, to allow the parting tool to be supported closer to the work.

21

22

22 Remember to allow the extra ¼in (6mm) when parting off.

23

23 Remove the cable ties and split the newspaper/glue joint to reveal the stepped interior. Twist one half through 90° and reassemble to produce the Art Deco shape.

24

24 The smaller diameter end faces have not yet been trimmed to size.

25

25 If any glue has squeezed through to the inside, carefully trim it away.

26

26 Sand the flat faces to remove the newspaper. Reposition the halves and mark the overlap on the small diameter end. Each half can be held flat on the table of a disc sander to trim the ends of the smaller diameter sections.

27 It is better to leave the smaller diameter ends long and trim to size rather than risk cutting slightly short.

27

28

28 A variety of internal shapes can be used. If other internal shapes are used, always consider the outer profile when planning the internal shape. It is very easy to misjudge and turn through from the outside into the hollow interior.

CHAPTER 11

MARBLE-RUN
STREPTOHEDRONS

MARBLE-RUN STREPTOHEDRONS

Here I will describe how to make a hexagon-based, streptohedron marble run. Once the technique is understood, any of the numerous forms of these twisted polygons and their hybrid shapes may be used. Consider also the possibility of arranging a central pivot between two halves, this would allow the channels to be moved, redirecting the ball bearings within. A puzzle could be produced, using the pivoted version, with coloured balls which have to be arranged in different sequences.

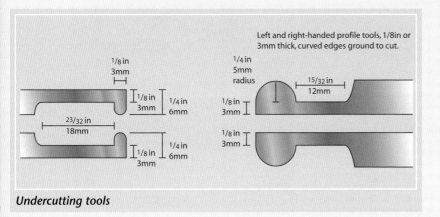

Undercutting tools

Special tools will be needed

Four special tools need to be ground from ¼in (6mm) wide by ⅛in (3mm) thick tool steel. Two are right-handed and the other two are left-handed. Nine ⅜in (9mm) diameter steel ball bearings will be needed.

Prepare a blank from two pieces of hardwood, here I have used yellow wood. The chosen wood needs to be close-grained for there are fine edges which could break out if an open-grained wood were used. Each half of the blank is 6in (150mm) long by 4in (100mm) wide by 2in (50mm) thick. Plane one face of each flat and true. Glue these two faces together, with newspaper between, to produce a finished blank 4in (100mm) square. If an expensive hardwood is used, to prevent waste at either end, prepare the central blank from the chosen wood and accurately glue (into prepared holes) dowels of a cheaper wood at either end.

The drawing provides the dimensions required. The outer shape is a hexagon. Once this basic profile has been turned the corners are turned away to allow for the grooves. Turning the basic shape is exactly as shown in Chapter 7.

The blank is turned, between chuck and cup centre, to an accurate 3¾in (96mm) diameter. To mark the centre line in pencil (B on the drawing), measure 3in (75mm) from the tailstock towards the headstock. From that centre line measure 1⅝in (41mm) towards the tailstock and mark, in pencil, line A. From the centre line (B) measure 1⅝in (41mm) towards the headstock and mark, in pencil, line C.

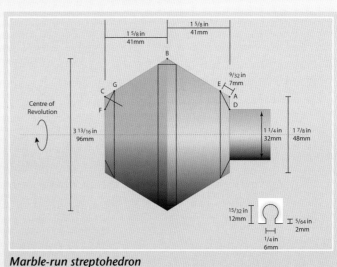

Marble-run streptohedron

Starting Work

1 On the tailstock side of line A turn down to an accurate 1¹⁵⁄₁₆in (48mm) diameter. Join the top of line B to the base of line A with a straight cut.

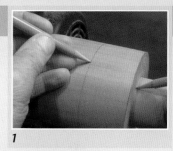

1

2

2 On the headstock side of line C turn down to 1⁷⁄₈in (48mm). Join the top of line B to the base of line C with a straight cut. Now, on the tailstock side of line A, turn down to 1¹⁄₄in (32mm) diameter.

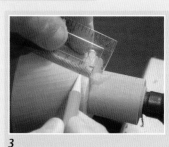

3

3 This now locates position D. Measure ⁹⁄₃₂in (7mm) from the corner of A up the slope towards B. Mark this position, line E.

4 Join positions D and E with a clean straight cut. Draw a centre line on this new face with pencil lines set ¹⁄₈in (3mm) either side of that centre line. A similar process is repeated around line C at the tailstock end to create the sloping face GF. Again mark the centre line on the newly turned face and pencil lines set ¹⁄₈in (3mm) either side of that centre line.

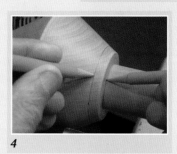

4

5 Next measure ⁹⁄₃₂in (7mm) from B towards A, then ⁹⁄₃₂in (7mm) from B towards C. Mark pencil lines.

5

6 Turn the flat face between these two newly marked pencil lines. Re-mark the centre line on this newly turned face. Mark pencil lines ¹⁄₈in (3mm) either side of this centre line.

6

Turning and Undercutting the Grooves

1 Take a ⅛in (3mm) wide square-end tool and make a white depth mark ½in (12mm) from its cutting edge. Using the square-end tool, set on a shelf toolrest with the tool cutting at centre height, turn a flat-bottomed groove in the ¼in (6mm) centrally marked area until the ½in (12mm) depth mark is reached.

So that the tool can be seen more clearly in some of the photographs, the toolrest has been covered with a non-reflective material. When using these four specially shaped tools **always** ensure that the cutting edge is angled **downwards**.

2 To undercut the turned groove, so that the ⅜in (9mm) diameter ball bearings will fit and run freely, take the left hand undercutting tool and place it at an angle on the toolrest as shown.

Angle the tool into the groove and gently scoop out an approximation of a ⅜in (9mm) internal curve on the left-hand side. Leave a small rim at the front edge unturned so that the edge will not crumble. Carefully remove the tool, following the pathway it took inwards.

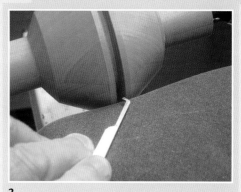

3 Take the right-hand undercutting tool, enter the groove at an angle, and gently scoop out an approximation of a ⅜in (9mm) internal curve on the right-hand side.

In the next series of photographs the specially ground profile tools, left and right-handed, are used to clean up the internal hollow. Again the toolrest has been covered in a non-reflective material so that the tool may be more clearly seen. Take note that the profile tool is fed into the groove with the cutting edge facing down. Once inside the groove, it is gently twisted upwards to cut the profile. Take light cuts.

4 The picture show the right-hand profile tool in use. The left-hand profile tool is used in the same way.

5 As a simple check, to ensure that the undercut pathway is correctly shaped, cut from card a lollipop shape with a 7/16in (11mm) diameter end. Fit this template in the hollowed groove and slowly rotate the work by hand. If the template runs freely in the groove all is fine, if it catches then make adjustments.

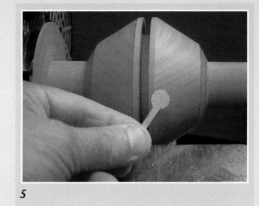

5

6 Now for the groove at the tailstock end. Set the shelf toolrest parallel to the area in which the groove is to be cut. Take the square-end tool and set it on the toolrest so that it is cutting at centre height. Point the tool towards the imagined centre of the work then turn a 1/2in (12mm) deep, flat-bottomed, groove between the two pencil lines which are set 1/4in (6mm) apart.

6

7 Take the left-hand undercutting tool and scoop out an approximation of the 3/8in (9mm) diameter hollow. Take the right-hand undercutting tool and scoop out an approximation of the 3/8in (9mm) diameter hollow.

7

8 Use the specially ground left and right-hand profile tools to clean out the hollow as described earlier, checking the shape with the card template. Sand and polish the part-finished half.

Gaining access to the area in which the groove is to be cut at the right-hand end is very difficult, so remove the piece from the chuck and reverse it in the lathe. Take care to ensure that it runs exactly on centre. Take the square-end tool and set it on the toolrest so that it is cutting at centre height. Point the tool towards the imagined centre of the work then turn a 1/2in (12mm) deep, flat-bottomed, groove between the two pencil lines which are set 1/4in (6mm) apart, exactly as before.

Take the left-hand undercutting tool and scoop out an approximation of the 3/8in (9mm) diameter hollow. Take the right-hand undercutting tool and scoop out an approximation of the 3/8in (9mm) diameter hollow.

8

9

9 Use the specially ground left and right-handed profile tools to clean out the hollow as described earlier, checking the shape with the card template. Sand and polish.

10 The piece may now be carefully parted off using a thin parting tool.

10

11 Split the newspaper/glue joint, then sand the newspaper surfaces flat and clean.

11

12 Check for fit, then drop the ³⁄₈in (9mm) diameter ball bearings into one of the channels in one half. Hold the two halves together and allow the balls to run around, checking all is well. Use a sanding disc to remove carefully any excess wood from the parted-off ends of each half.

Slide the nine ball bearings into one half, then carefully glue the two halves together, holding the joint with masking tape whilst the glue dries. If there are any steps in the groove joints, which may slow the ball bearings, use a flexible drive shaft with a round dental burr to gently ease out the bumps.

Why not try a marble run in one of the branched versions of the streptohedron (Chapter 9)? I have not tried one yet, yours may be a first.

12

CHAPTER 12

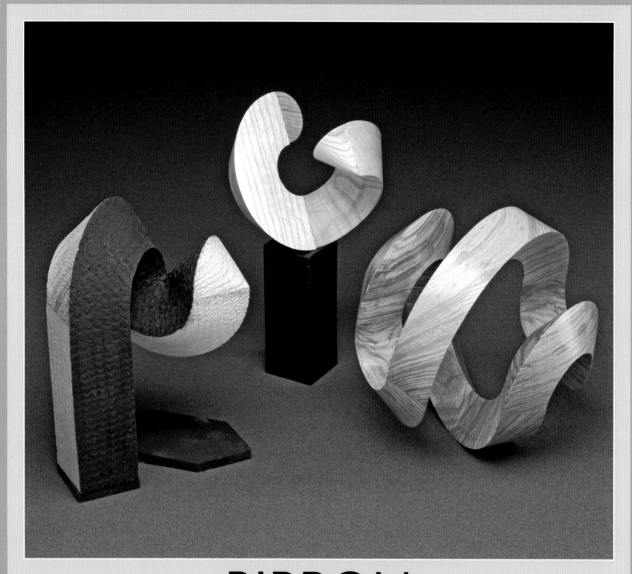

RIBBON
STREPTOHEDRONS

RIBBON STREPTOHEDRONS

John Sharp (a mathematician friend), when looking at the streptohedrons that I had produced, asked, 'What would these forms look like if they were hollowed, if they had no centre?' At the time I felt that it would be impossible to turn away the centres of the streptohedrons, how would they be held when being worked? It seemed a nice idea but did

he understand what he was asking me to do? The answer to this problem, like many others, came to me in the night. It was clear and so obvious. As can be seen from the drawing below, the pieces may be made up from a series of turned rings which when split can be twisted and rejoined in exactly the same way as solid streptohedrons.

What you will need

- A 3in (75mm) long, $\frac{1}{4}$in (6mm) carriage bolt with nut and washer.
- A 9in (230mm) diameter by $^{13}/_{16}$in
- (20mm) thick plywood disc.
  Three blanks. The wood I have used is olive ash.

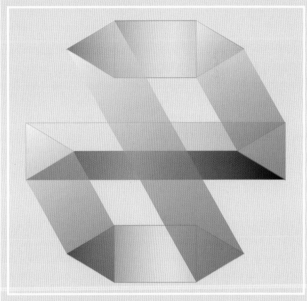

Design for a ribbon streptohedron

Preparation

The first blank is made from two pieces of wood each $6^{3}/_{8}$in (160mm) long by $3^{3}/_{16}$in (80mm) wide by $1^{9}/_{16}$in (40mm) thick. The other two blanks are made from two pieces $4^{3}/_{4}$in (120mm) long by $2^{3}/_{8}$in (60mm) wide by $1^{9}/_{16}$in (40mm) thick. They are joined along their centre lines with a newspaper/glue joint. Make sure that the top surfaces are flat and true.

When the glue has dried, from the first blank cut a $6^{3}/_{8}$in (160mm) diameter circle and drill at its centre (and precisely on the newspaper/glue line) a $\frac{1}{4}$in (6mm) hole. From the other two blanks cut $4^{3}/_{4}$in (120mm) circles and at their centres (and precisely on the newspaper/glue lines) drill a $\frac{1}{4}$in (6mm) hole. The picture shows the blanks.

Turning the largest rings

Fit the plywood disc centrally onto a metal faceplate. Turn the edge clean. At the centre of the disc drill a 1/4in (6mm) hole.

Remove the disc from the faceplate. Mark a datum on the back of the disc and on the faceplate so that it may be accurately realigned. Fit the carriage bolt into the hole through the back of the disc. Tap the bolt head so that the locating square (under the head) is pressed into the plywood. Refit the disc to the faceplate and the faceplate to the lathe. The threaded section of the bolt should be facing out.

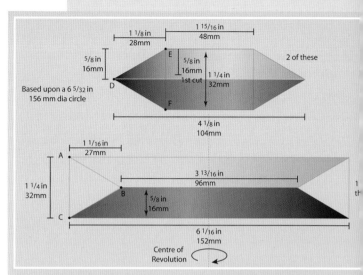

Based upon a 6 5/32 in 156 mm dia circle

1 1/8 in 28mm
1 15/16 in 48mm
5/8 in 16mm
5/8 in 16mm
1 1/4 in 32mm
1st cut
2 of these
D
E
F
4 1/8 in 104mm

1 1/16 in 27mm
A
1 1/4 in 32mm
B
3 13/16 in 96mm
5/8 in 16mm
C
6 1/16 in 152mm

Centre of Revolution

Equal-sided triangular cross-section ribbon based on hexagon

1 Take the largest blank and fit the central 1/4in (6mm) hole over the coach bolt. Push the knock-out bar through the headstock to prevent the bolt from being pushed out of the disc. Fit a washer and nut on the thread and tighten with a wrench. This single nut and bolt, when tightened down, is sufficient to hold the work securely whilst turning. The underside of the blank **must** be perfectly flat, otherwise the pressure applied from the bolt could open the newspaper/glue joint.

Turn the front face flat and true. Take as small a cut as possible, because when the blank is reversed if the central area around the bolt is raised the blank will not seat firmly. On that front face mark a 6 1/16in (152mm) diameter pencil circle. Move the toolrest to the side of the work and turn the edge down to that marked pencil line. Make sure that the edge is flat and square to the front face. Sand and polish the edge.

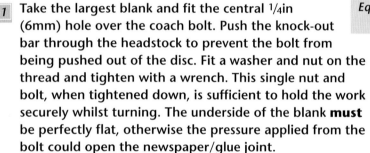

1

2 On the face of the work mark a 3 13/16in (96mm) diameter pencil circle.

2

3 On the inside of that marked line turn in accurately, using a square-end tool, to a depth of 5/8in (16mm). This will position point B. A shelf toolrest supports the tool and a white correction fluid mark on the tool marks the depth of the cut.

3

4 The outer rim of the turned blank which is closest to the turner is line A. Now join line A to line B with a clean sloping cut. Use a straightedge to check that the slope is flat then sand and polish.

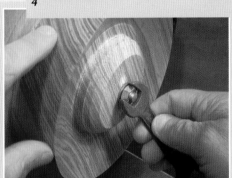

5 Undo the nut and remove the blank from the plywood faceplate. Reverse the blank and fit it onto the carriage bolt and tighten the nut. It is important to make sure that the blank runs on centre. If it does not, then loosen the nut and rotate the blank a small distance and try again until it runs on centre. If this does not work then find the high spot, loosen the nut and push the high spot to bring the work to centre.

6 Measure, 1¼in (32mm) along the turned face from where the blank touches the plywood faceplate, and mark a pencil line. Turn the face of the work down to this line, flat and true, bringing the blank to the correct thickness.

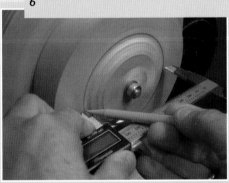

7 On that turned face mark a 3¹³/₁₆in (96mm) diameter pencil circle. Cut six softwood blocks 1³/₁₆in (30mm) by 1in (25mm) square. Drill and countersink down through the square end to accept a 2in (50mm) long screw. These blocks will help hold the turned disc once it has been parted through.

8 Take one of the softwood blocks and press it firmly against the side face of the disc. Push the screw in and screw down. Fit the other five blocks around the edge of the turned blank. These blocks, by themselves, are not sufficient to hold the blank in place once it has been turned and parted through. Secure them against the blank using tacks of hot-melt glue. These glue tacks will hold the blank to the blocks yet are easily removed, without leaving a mark, when the work is complete.

9 As a safety precaution, rotate the lathe by hand before switching on. Using a shelf toolrest to support the square-end tool, turn on the inside of the marked 3¹³/₁₆in (96mm) pencil circle to a depth of ⁵/₈in (16mm). Make sure that the cut is square to the face of the work. This turned hollow should meet up with the cut from the opposite side.

9

10 Once the work has been parted through, the centre core and the carriage bolt may be removed.

10

11 Point C now has to be joined to the inner rim of the hollow (point B in the diagram on page 150) as shown in the photograph. Turn a flat face between these two points.

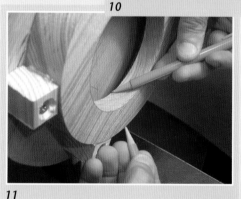

11

12 Check with a straightedge to make sure the turned face is flat. Sand and polish that face.

12

13 When satisfied with the piece, the softwood supporting blocks may be removed. Unscrew and pull the blocks away. The hot melt-glue will pull away from the polished surface leaving little or no mark. The finished ring may be set aside.

13

Turning the two smaller rings

Both smaller rings are turned in exactly the same manner. Fit the blank onto the carriage bolt, turn the face flat removing as little as possible, next mark a 4⅛in (104mm) diameter pencil circle on the face of the work. Turn the outer edge down to that marked pencil line, making sure that it is square to the face. On the face of the work mark another pencil circle, this time 1¹⁵/₁₆in (48mm) diameter. This is line E. (See the illustration on page 150.)

1

2

1 On the inside of this pencil circle, using a square-end tool supported upon a shelf toolrest, turn down to a depth of ⅝in (16mm). Make sure that this hollow cut is square to the face.

3

2 On the edge face, measure, from the top face of the blank, ⅝in (16mm) and, at this point, mark a pencil line on the edge. This will be line D. (See page 150)

3 Now join line D to line E with a straight, clean cut. Check the slope with a straightedge.

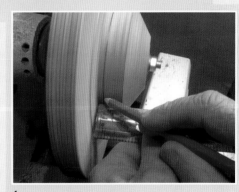

4

4 From line D measure a further ⅝in (16mm) and mark a pencil line. This is line F. Sand and polish the sloping face and a little of the inside hollow.

5 Loosen the nut and remove the blank from the carriage bolt.

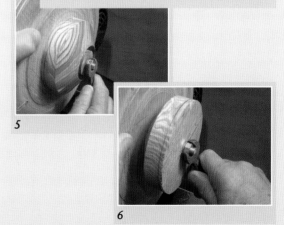

5

6 Turn the blank over and refit onto the carriage bolt, making sure that the blank runs exactly on centre. Turn the face down to the pencil line (line F), which will bring the blank to the correct thickness, then mark a 1¹⁵/₁₆in (48mm) diameter pencil circle on the face of the work.

6

7 On the inside of that marked pencil circle turn in, using a square-end tool supported on a shelf toolrest, to a depth of ¼in (6mm) but do not part through. Join the edge of the turned hollow to line D with a straight clean cut, checking the slope with a straightedge. Sand and polish the sloping face.

7

8 Cut four softwood blocks, with a 60° cutout, to be screwed around the turned blank for support. Secure these blocks to the blank using hot-melt glue tacks.

8

9 Continue to turn out the internal hollow until the tool breaks through to the hollow beneath, then remove the central core and the carriage bolt.

9

10 Make sure that the internal hollow is exactly 1¹⁵/₁₆in (48mm) all the way through to the faceplate. Sand and polish. In the picture the hollow is being sanded with abrasive paper wrapped around a stick. Polish the hollow using a cloth securely wrapped around a dowel.

10

11 When satisfied, remove the piece from the plywood faceplate. Turn the remaining blank in exactly the same way.

11

12 The picture shows the parts waiting for their newspaper/glue joints to be split.

12

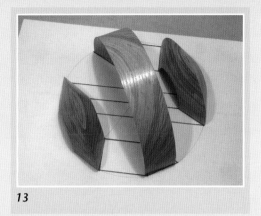

13

13 If the halves of the split rings are arranged upon the drawing it will be seen how they will fit once they have been twisted. Before the halves are glued together, rub the glued newspaper away from the join line on a flat sheet of glasspaper.

14 The parts are glued together and held in place, whilst the glue sets, with masking tape. When fixing the parts together, if there is any mismatch, make sure that the internal curves are aligned first. External curves are far easier to clean up than the internal curves. A miniature drum sander is a most useful tool and can be used to clean up the joints.

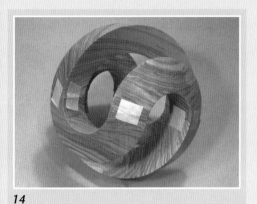

14

15 There are endless forms to explore. In the version described above, the cross-section is a triangle with equal sides. The triangular cross-section points towards the centre. Look at the picture the two forms are based on a hexagonal alignment, they both have triangular cross-sectional ribbons but the one on the left has the triangular cross-section facing outwards, the one on the right has the triangle facing inwards. Other polygonal forms (or shapes such as oblongs) may be used as a cross-section. Also consider shapes with a Y or X cross-section or the five or six branched forms described in Chapter 9.

The form described above is based around a hexagon with the rotational centre through the flats. Try one with the centre of rotation through the points, next try a hybrid of the parts. Try a five-sided form (see the yew ram's horn ribbon form on the frontispiece). Professor Johannes Volmer has turned some of these ribbons elliptically. They are most interesting and of course hybrids can be made of those forms using a mixture of round and elliptical. Bob Rollings has turned a delightful small ribbon form (62mm or 2¹/₂in overall diameter), so smaller pieces work just as well as larger ones.

Of course there is the possibility of using curved sides and edges. I have not tried turning curves on these ribbons yet but I have had a form made for me using rapid prototyping which has produced startling shapes. (See the white snowflake type form in the Gallery) I hope that you will experiment, spectacular results await you.

15

The finished item

Cone Ribbon Form

This ribbon form is the easiest and most effective shape to turn. Just one simple turned ring can create several unusual shapes. Choose wood with spectacular grain for a classical look, or use plain and simple wood which allows the form to be spray-painted. Elevate the finished piece, place it on a stand, it needs to be raised so that the movement of the form may be appreciated.

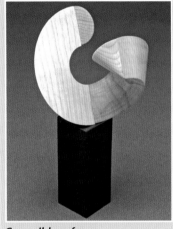

Cone ribbon form

What you will need

- A metal faceplate with a 5in (125mm) diameter by 1in (25mm) thick softwood disc attached.
- A shelf toolrest.
- A ¹/₈in (3mm) wide square-end tool.
- Two pieces of wood each 4³/₄in (120mm) long by 2³/₈in (60mm) wide by 1³/₈in (35mm) thick.
- Two pieces of wood each 3in (75mm) long by 1⁹/₁₆in (40mm) wide by ³/₄in (20mm) thick from which to turn the (split) cone.
- A 1¹/₄in (30mm) sawtooth drill bit.

1 Using a newspaper/glue joint, fix the two larger pieces of wood together to make a blank 4³/₄in (120mm) square. When the joint is dry, plane one face flat and true. Cut a 4³/₄in (120mm) diameter circle from the blank with the centre point, P, on the joint line. Apply white PVA wood glue to the planed surface of the blank and to the wood faceplate. Place a sheet of newspaper on the glued surface of the wood facepate and press the glued surface of the blank onto it.

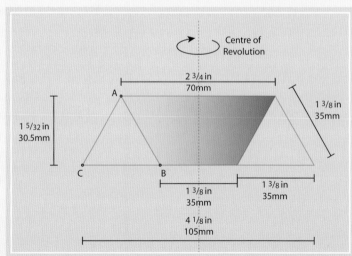

1   Cross-section of the piece. It will be noticed that an equal-sided 35mm (1³/₈in) triangular doughnut is about to be turned

2 Bring the revolving centre forward and press it into point P (the centre of the blank). When the glue has gripped the work, and there is no chance of slippage, withdraw the revolving centre a short way and place a larger piece of wood between the centre and the work. Press the centre into this wood and apply pressure to the blank. This will spread the pressure on the blank evenly whilst the glue dries.

3 When the glue has dried, turn the outer edge of the blank to a cylinder. On that outer edge measure and mark a line $1^3/_{16}$in (30.5mm) away from the wood faceplate.

4 Turn the face down, flat and true, to the marked pencil line. On that face initially mark two pencil circles. The first is $4^5/_{32}$in (105mm) diameter, line C; and the second is $1^3/_8$in (35mm) diameter, line B.

5 Turn the outer edge down to the $4^5/_{32}$in (105mm) diameter pencil line. Where the edge of the blank touches the wood faceplate is line C. Next mark a $2^3/_4$in (70mm) diameter pencil circle on the face of the work. This is line A.

Fit the $1^1/_4$in (30mm) sawtooth drill into a Jacobs drill chuck at the tailstock and drill to a depth of $1^3/_{16}$in (30.5mm). Using a square-end tool, supported on a shelf toolrest and cutting at centre height, turn out the drilled hole to the marked $1^3/_8$in (35mm) pencil circle.

6 Make sure that the sides of the hole are cut square to the front face. Where the inside edge of the hole meets the wood faceplate is line B.

7 Now join line B to line A with a straight clean cut.

8 Next join lines A and C with a straight clean cut. Sand and polish the sloping faces.

2

3

4

5

6

7

8

9 The piece may now be removed from the wood faceplate. Split the newspaper/glue joint between the blank and the faceplate. To prevent damaging the planed face of the blank, use wood wedges once the joint has been partially opened. The newspaper that is still attached to the work can be carefully sanded off on a sheet of glasspaper resting on a flat surface.

10 Split the joint holding the two halves of the ring to expose the equal-sided triangular cross-section. The halves may be twisted and rejoined to form a variety of sculptural shapes.

11 Turn a small cone with a 1³/₁₈in (35mm) equal sided triangular cross-section. See Chapter 7 page 66. If a newspaper/glue joint is set on the centre line it may be split into two half cones.

12 These will fit neatly over the exposed triangular ends of the glued-up parts. The picture shows the piece turned from tiger maple.

13 In this version the wood has been sprayed black and, using powerful rare earth magnets, steel ball bearings have been attached.

14 For those who find the mathematical side of this project of interest in the picture the pieces have been assembled into a twisted conical form. The negative space within this twisted form is hexagonal (length of side 1³/₈in or 35m) itself a twisted form, a streptohedron.

These are most satisfying pieces to turn. There is a relationship between the triangular cross-section and the hollow in the centre. Try increasing the centre hollow, turn these large, turn them with bark-included edges – be inventive. If three rings are turned of different diameters but with the same triangular cross-section they can be split and re-joined to produce a ribbon form *similar* to that described above.

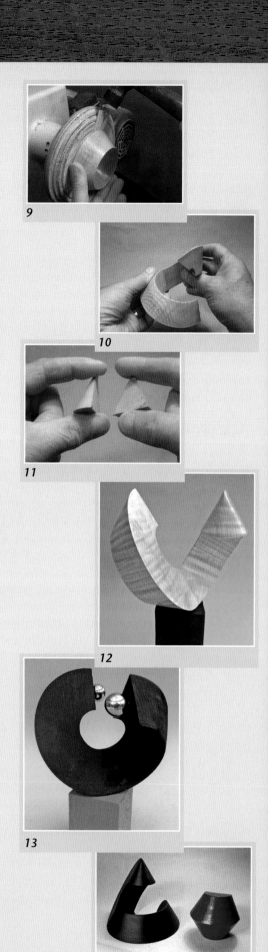

Ribbon Knot

Consider the many axes in which a square can be rotated: with the axis along the diagonal producing a double cone (the sphericon), with the axis on the centre line across the flat faces producing a cylinder, with the axis along one edge producing a wide cylinder and with the axis on one corner producing a ring with a square cross-section. This last form is of interest because, when the split parts are reassembled, it may be used to create twists, almost knots, in wood.

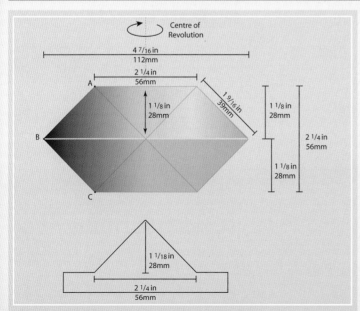

Knot ribbon form

What you will need

- A 6in (150mm) faceplate with a 6in (150mm) diameter, 1in (25mm) thick softwood disc attached.
- A shelf toolrest.
- Two pieces of wood (here I am using ash) 4³/₄in (120mm) long by 2³/₈in (60mm) square. These are joined together with a newspaper/glue joint to produce a blank which is 4³/₄in (120mm) square and 2³/₈in (60mm) thick.
- A slicing tool as shown on page 84.
- Four 3in (75mm) long screws.
- Two pieces of ash 4in (100mm) long by 2³/₈in (60mm) by 30mm (1³/₁₆in). These are joined together with a newspaper/glue joint to produce a blank 4in (100mm) long by 2³/₈in (60mm) square. From this is turned a sphericon.

The drawing and template provide all the necessary dimensions. From the larger prepared blank cut a 4³/₈in (120mm) circle. Accurately mark the centre along the glue line. Using a newspaper/glue joint fix this blank onto the wood faceplate, pressing the revolving centre into its marked centre.

When the glue has dried, turn the outer edge down, bringing the blank to an accurate 4⁷/₁₆in (112mm) diameter. Turn the face flat and true and on that face mark a 2⁷/₃₂in (56mm) pencil circle. This will be line A.

Centre of Revolution

4 7/16 in
112mm

2 1/4 in
56mm

A

1 1/8 in
28mm

1 9/16 in
39mm

1 1/8 in
28mm

B

2 1/4 in
56mm

1 1/8 in
28mm

C

1 1/18 in
28mm

2 1/4 in
56mm

Cross-section of the square knot plus a template

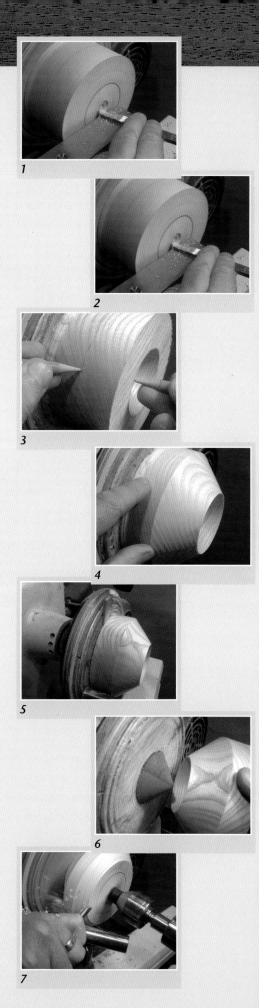

1 From the front edge measure 1⅛in (28mm) along the side and mark a pencil line. This will be line B.

Fit the shelf toolrest in the toolpost, raising it so that the slicing tool will cut at centre height.

1

2

2 Begin to slice from the centre into the face of the work. Check the shape of the hollow using the template shown on page 159. Continue to turn out the conical hollow, making adjustments where necessary, until the template is an exact fit.

3 In the picture lines A and B are indicated. Use a sharp gouge to join these two positions with a clean, straight cut.

3

4 Sand and polish if the piece is to have a fully polished finish.

4

5 Once this turned edge has been sanded, split the newspaper/glue joint attaching the blank to the faceplate, first using a sharp knife, then a wood wedge.

5

6 Glue a small piece of scrap wood to the wood faceplate. When the glue has dried, turn this block down to a conical shape to match the hollow turned in the face of the work. This turned cone will ensure that the blank is held on centre. Bring a cup centre, held in the tailstock, forward and press it against the marked centre of the now reversed blank. Make adjustments if necessary to ensure that the blank runs on centre. Mark a 2⁷⁄₃₂in (56mm) diameter pencil circle on the face of the work. This is line C.

6

7 Now join line C to line B with a clean, straight cut. When satisfied, sand the sloping side.

7

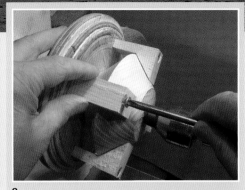

8

8 The pressure from the cup centre prevents the blank from moving on the wood faceplate. So that the centre may be withdrawn, allowing the conical hollow to be turned into the blank, cut four softwood supports. These supports have an angled face which matches the 45° angled edge of the blank. Drill down through these supports so that they may be screwed down around the outer edge of the blank. To make sure that the blank is securely held use tacks of hot-melt glue. The conical hollow may now be turned into the face of the work. Use exactly the same method as described earlier when turning the conical hollow in the opposite face.

9

9 When the conical hollow has been sanded (and polished if required), the blank may be removed from the faceplate.

10

10 Split the newspaper/glue joint, to expose the turned profile. Turn a Sphericon (see Chapter 7 Double Cone, page 70) with a side length of 1⁹/₁₆in (39mm) which will match half of the profile that has been turned.

11

11 Now try the split sphericon halves on the split blank to see the shapes that are created. A shape with only one side may be produced by fitting the half double cones onto the blank with one half set at right angles to the other. Trace the sides with your finger and if the half-sphericons are set correctly the start and finish points connect. The sphericon halves will also fit into the conical hollows in the blank to create a larger double cone or sphericon.

12

12 Finally, glue the parts together to create the knot form. In the picture the pieces are held together with masking tape while the glue dries. The piece here is not polished because I intend to texture the surface. See Brid and Ambrose O'Halloran's knot form in the Gallery, page 185.

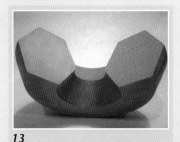

13

13 The cross-section of the turned ring can be any shape you like as long as it has rotational symmetry, allowing the piece to be cut, twisted and rejoined. This picture shows a ring with a hexagonal cross-section. And don't forget that pieces may be turned on different axes and hybrid forms can also be made.

CHAPTER 13

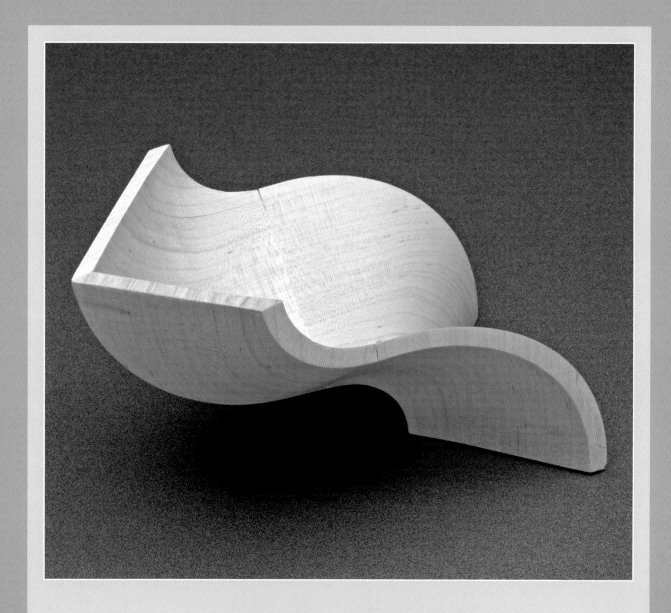

WAVE BOWL

WAVE BOWL

The production of the wave bowl, shown left, uses some of the techniques described earlier but additional cutting and reassembly are involved. This provides a more practical finished product, a bowl. Although cutting and reassembling turned forms is not a new idea, this particular piece is very interesting because it relies upon a very controlled turned shape, allowing the production of a precise and controlled finished piece.

What you will need

■ Two pieces of hardwood, here I am using maple, each piece 7^{1}/$_{16}$in (180mm) long by 3^{17}/$_{32}$in (90mm) wide by 2in (50mm) thick with their long narrow edges planed flat and true.

■ An 8in (200mm) diameter by ^{1}/$_{2}$in (12mm) thick plywood disc.

■ A 3in (75mm) long, ^{1}/$_{4}$in (6mm) diamveter bolt and nut from which to make a central bolt and captive-nut chuck as described in Chapter 2.

■ A ^{1}/$_{8}$in (3mm) wide square-end tool.

■ A shelf toolrest.

■ An accurate drawing as shown below.

Preparation

Take the two pieces of hardwood and join the long narrow edges together using a newspaper/glue joint to make a blank 7^{1}/$_{16}$in (180mm) square. When the glue has dried measure along the joint line and mark its centre.

Place the point of a pencil compass, set to 3^{17}/$_{32}$in (90mm) radius, on that marked centre and draw a circle.

Use a bandsaw to cut the marked circle. At the marked centre of the now circular blank, drill a hole to accept the ^{1}/$_{4}$in (6mm) bolt.

Fix the blank to the prepared plywood disc with a newspaper/glue joint, locking it firmly down by tightening the bolt. Leave until the newspaper/glue joint is fully dry.

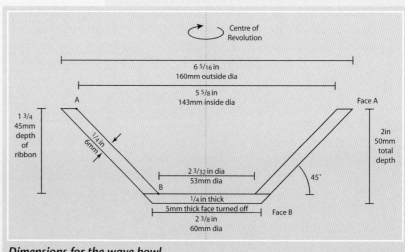

Dimensions for the wave bowl

Turning the Piece

When the joint is dry the bolt may be removed so that face A may be turned flat and true. Mark a concentric $2^3/_{32}$in (53mm) diameter pencil circle on the face of the work.

1 Mark two further concentric pencil circles, the first $6^5/_{16}$ in (160mm) diameter. and the second $5^5/_8$in (143mm) diameter. Turn the blank to the marked $6^5/_{16}$in (160mm) diameter. Take the $^1/_8$in (3mm) wide square-end tool and mark, using typists' correction fluid, a position $1^3/_4$in (45mm) from the cutting edge.

2 On the inside of the $2^3/_{32}$in (53mm) marked pencil circle accurately turn to a depth of $1^3/_4$in (45mm) using the square-end tool supported on a shelf toolrest and cutting at centre height.

3 Now join the base of the centrally turned hollow to the edge of the $5^5/_8$in (143mm) diameter marked pencil circle with a straight cut.

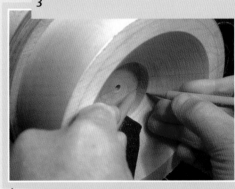

4 Whilst turning this sloping face, to help judge whether the angle is correct, check the width of the uncut area at the base of the slope against the width of the uncut area adjoining the marked pencil circle.

5 If they are the same, then the angle of the slope is correct and work may continue. If it is smaller at the base than the top then the angle is too steep. If larger at the base than the top then the angle is too shallow. Adjustments may then be made to produce the correct slope. The angled face must be flat and true. When satisfied, sand and polish the angled face but not the edge.

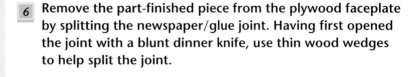

6

6 Remove the part-finished piece from the plywood faceplate by splitting the newspaper/glue joint. Having first opened the joint with a blunt dinner knife, use thin wood wedges to help split the joint.

7

7 The work is now reversed upon the plywood faceplate using a newspaper/glue joint to hold the work firmly. Make sure that the work runs on centre before the bolt is fully tightened, then allow the glue to dry. On the now top face, mark a 2³/₈in (60mm) diameter pencil circle. If the blank is thinner (or thicker) than 2in (50mm), then this diameter may be different. To calculate the required diameter measure the thickness of the blank and transfer that measurement to the drawing from face A towards face B. Draw a line parallel to face A at this position. The measured distance between the sloping sides where this new line cuts them will be the required diameter.

8

8 Join the base of the blank (where it is fixed to the plywood faceplate) to the marked pencil circle on face B with a clean straight cut. Sand and polish the sloping edge.

9

9 Unscrew the bolt and begin to turn the top face. Gently turn until the hollow beneath is exposed.

10

10 Turn the face flat and true. Carefully split the newspaper/glue joint, opening it first with a blunt knife and then using fine wood wedges.

11 The picture shows half the turned piece released from the faceplate. Place a piece of sandpaper on a flat surface and carefully rub the remnants of the newspaper and glue away.

12 For fun, try fitting the halves together to see the variety of shapes that may be made.

13 Using the bandsaw, accurately cut the halves into quarters.

14 These can make more shapes.

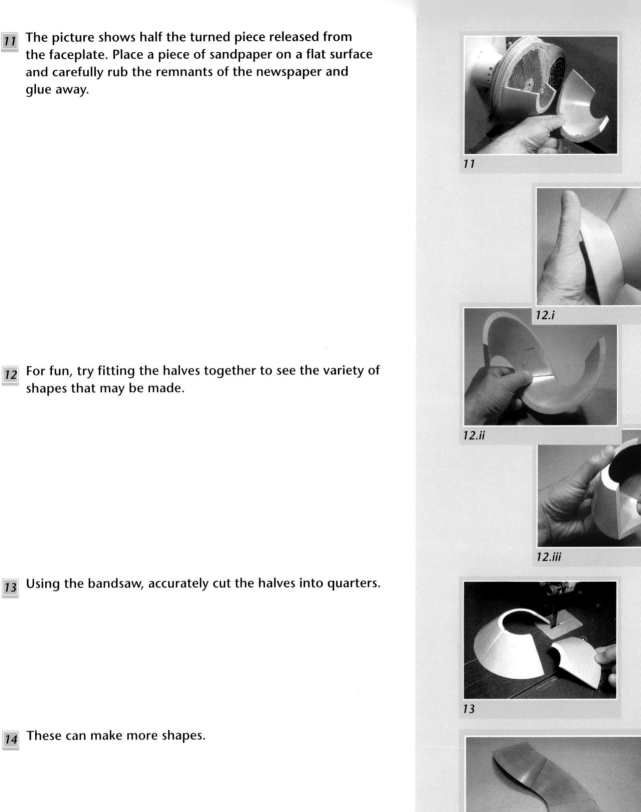

11

12.i

12.ii

12.iii

13

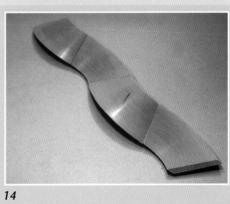

14

15

15 Glue two quarters, small side to small side, and the other two, long side to long side. Hold them in place using masking tape whilst the glue dries. White carpenter's glue will provide good adhesion as side grain is being joined to side grain.

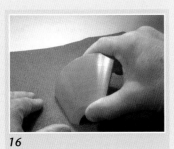

16

16 When the glue has dried, carefully sand the end faces of each piece. The two parts may now be glued together to make the wave bowl. Before gluing the two parts, test them for fit. If the fit is good, go ahead and glue them; if the fit is not perfectly aligned (this will happen more often than a perfect fit), do not be dismayed. It is more important to arrange the pieces so that the inner edges are as close as possible, because they are the edges which will be more difficult to clean up.

17

17 Polyurethane glue is used to join the endgrain faces as it provides an exceptionally strong bond. Apply the glue, line up the edges and hold the parts together using masking tape whilst the glue dries.

18

18 If the joint was not perfectly aligned it may be cleaned and smoothed into a flowing curve using sandpaper or a rotary sanding drum as seen in the picture. Make sure that the surface is sanded smooth before applying any finish.

19

19 The picture shows part of the finished piece. Here maple was the chosen wood so that the form could be clearly seen. Try exotic woods and see how these more flamboyant woods can enhance this wave form. Pablo Nemzoff has decorated a wave bowl – see the Gallery section.

CHAPTER 14

TURNING SQUARE HOLES

This remarkably simple yet effective piece of turning proves that just about any shape can be turned on the lathe.

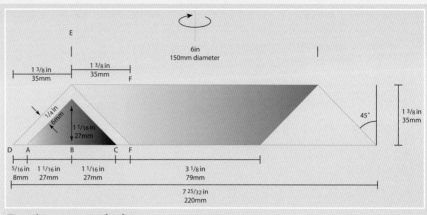

Turning square holes

What you will need

- A 10in (250mm) diameter by 1⁹/₁₆in (40mm) thick hardwood disc. Here I am using ash.
- A 10in (250mm) diameter by ¹/₂in (12mm) thick plywood disc.
- A 3in (75mm) long, ¹/₄in (6mm) diameter carriage bolt, nut and washer from which to make a carriage-bolt chuck as described in Chapter 2.
- A shelf toolrest.
- A slicing tool as described on page 84.
- An accurate drawing as shown above.

Preparation

Drill a ¹/₄in (6mm) hole at the centre of the hardwood blank. The blank may, if you wish, have a newspaper/glue joint along the centre line. Here I am using a single piece of wood. Slide the hardwood blank onto the centrally placed carriage bolt in the plywood disc and tighten down the nut. Now turn the edge of the blank clean and square. Turn the face of the blank so that it is flat and true, removing as little as possible from this top surface. From the outer edge of the blank, measure and make pencil lines at the following distances: ⁵/₁₆in (8mm) for line A. From line A, towards the centre, 1¹/₁₆in (27mm) for line B. From line B, towards the centre, a further 1¹/₁₆in (27mm) for line C. Take the slicing tool, (see page 84), and mark upon its shank a position 1¹/₁₆in (27mm) from its tip.

1. Using the slicing tool (see page 84), supported on a shelf toolrest and cutting at centre height, begin to cut into the face of the work on the left of line B. The cut at line B must remain vertical, for below this position is the base of the vee cut forming the square hole. Use a gouge to remove some of the waste wood to the right of line B, but leave some of the vertical side of line B as a marker.

2. Continue slicing the angled side and test with the template (i) making adjustments to the cut until the template fits.

3. Next turn from line C down to line B, until the template (ii) is a perfect fit. Clean up the inside surface but do not round over any of the sharp edges. If the completed piece is to have a polished finish, sand and polish this surface now. Do not polish the top edge, for this will be glued later. Undo the nut from the carriage bolt and remove the work from the plywood disc. The small raised area around the centre hole needs to be cut away with a chisel. This will allow the blank to sit flat and firm on the plywood disc when it is repositioned.

4. Use a newspaper/glue joint to fix the blank onto the plywood disc, tightening the nut upon the carriage bolt. This should bring the work onto centre. Switch on the lathe to make sure that it is on centre. **Adjust if necessary**. Leave until the glue has dried.

5. Turn the face of the work flat and true, bringing the blank to 1³⁄₈in (35mm) thick.

On the face of the work measure from the edge towards the centre, first 1³⁄₈in (35mm) to mark line E, then a further 1³⁄₈in (35mm) to mark line F. Now join line E to the outer base edge of the blank with a straight clean cut.

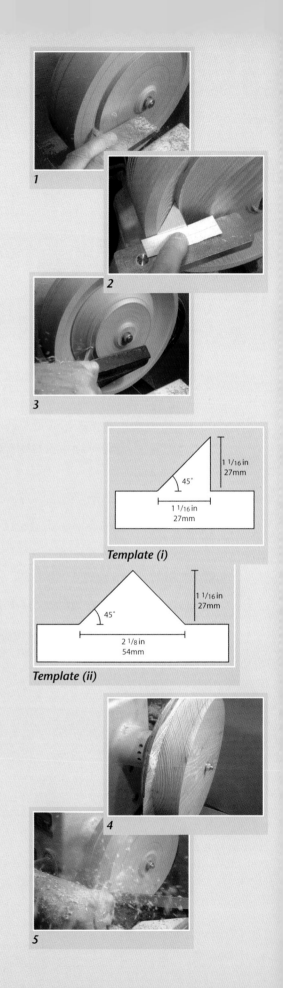

Template (i)

1 1/16 in
27mm

45°

1 1/16 in
27mm

Template (ii)

1 1/16 in
27mm

45°

2 1/8 in
54mm

6 Use a square-end tool to turn, on the inside of line F, to the full depth of the blank. Undo the nut from the carriage bolt and remove the central core.

7 Join line E to the base of line F. Make sure that the sloping face is flat and true. Sand both the cut faces (and polish if that is the chosen finish), then split the newspaper/glue joint. Use wood wedges so that the split face is not damaged. Clean off the newspaper on the split face by rubbing the work on a sheet of glasspaper.

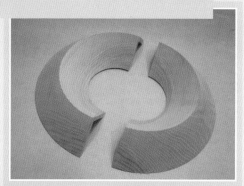

8 Take the blank to the bandsaw and cut it across the centre.

9 The two halves can now be joined together, revealing the turned 'square' hole. Hold them with masking tape whilst the glue sets.

10 Draw on card two circles, matching the outer and inner diameters of the blank. Use a protractor to mark five radiating lines 30 degrees apart. Cut through these radiating lines. **It is important that these lines (you may choose how many you wish to make) radiate from the centre of the turned curves so that the cross-section, when cut, will be of a regular shape allowing the parts to be rejoined in a variety of configurations.**

11 These segments are used to mark guidelines on the joined blank.

11

12 Take the blank to the bandsaw and cut through the pencil guidelines. The cut must be made towards the perceived centre of the curve so that a regular square cross-section is produced. This will allow the cut parts to be reassembled in different orientations, providing the largest variation of twists. Leave the last two segments uncut.

12

13 The segments may be rejoined, twisting each segment as they are glued in place, to make this turned vessel with a turned square hole. I used polyurethane glue to fix the segments together, as end grain was being glued to end grain.

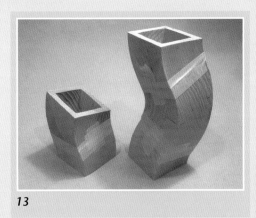

13

14 Whilst the glue dries, the parts are held together using masking tape. Clean up the outer and inner faces using a small rotary drum sander. To add interest to this twisted form I have finished the piece with texture and colour. The picture shows the piece coloured but with the texture yet to be applied.

Here a square hole with a square outer profile has been turned. Use your imagination, for other hollow shapes may be turned within: round holes are an easy option. Consider the outer form also: triangular, pentagonal or hexagonal shapings are possible. The alignment of the outer shapes to the axis of rotation can also differ, so in some cases hybrid forms could be produced. There are just so many variations and alternatives that there must be an endless variety of these unusual, fully turned, twisted vessels.

14

A Simple Guide to Spray-Finishing Work

I use automotive spray paints to colour the work, so ensure there is adequate ventilation and a mask is worn at all times. Read the instructions on the can. Spraying must take place in a dust-free atmosphere, so either work first thing in the morning or work away from your turning area. The work should be contained within a spray booth to prevent mists of colour settling on other areas. A large cardboard box works well.

1

The method I use is extremely simple. The surface of the work must be clean and free of dust and grease. The surface must be well finished for the spray finish will not mask problem areas, in fact it will accentuate any faults.

2

1 Begin with a good primer coat, grey primer for dark colours, white for lighter. Generally, I like the grain to show through the spray finish so I spray a thin coat of primer. If the final finish is to be a solid bright colour then a dense primer coat is needed. Leave to dry overnight. Lightly sand the surface then spray with the chosen coloured spray. Leave to dry. Apply further coats of spray paint if necessary. I like to mask off areas and spray different colours so here is how I prepare the work. Having spray-primed the surface, the whole piece is covered with masking tape, inside and out. Draw the chosen shapes on the surface of the masking tape.

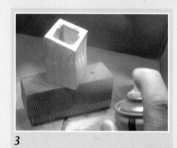

3

2 Use a sharp scalpel to cut carefully along the pencil lines. Peel off the masking tape to expose the areas to be coloured.

4

3 Spray with the chosen colour. Leave the sprayed coat to dry.

4 When the paint has dried, peel off the masking tape to expose the finished surface. And don't worry, if you don't like the finished effect just sand down, spray another primer coat and start again.

5

5 Colouring work in this manner opens up whole new vistas. The picture shows a few part-finished pieces, some about to have texture added, others about to have more colour added.

CHAPTER 15

NAUTILUS

1 The natural spiral of a nautilus shell is so very satisfying. It flows so well, curling in upon itself.

This spiral is based on a series of numbers called the Fibonacci numbers: 0, 1, 1, 2, 3, 5, 8, 13, 21 etc. where each number is the sum of the two preceding numbers. If these numbers are arranged as a series of squares then a spiral can be created by drawing arcs which connect the opposite corners of those squares.

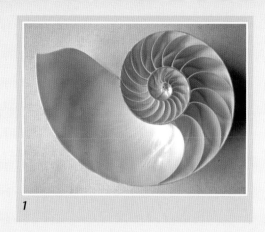

1

2 If a series of square-sided bowls are turned, each of a diameter relating to a Fibonacci number, they can be split and rejoined to create this Nautilus spiral. In each case the bowl blank has a newspaper/glue joint running across its diameter. This will allow the finished bowl to be split accurately in half when complete. Each bowl, although having different diameters, will have the same wall and base thickness. Here I am using maple from which to turn the bowls. The choice is yours, you may even use two different woods joined at the newspaper/glue line and from those blanks two Nautilus vessels may be created.

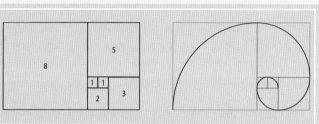

Above: A series of squares are laid out in the proportions shown: 1, 1, 2, 3, 5, 8 etc.
Above right: To create the spiral, draw an arc in each square, connecting the opposing corners.

There will be six parts for this vessel and their diameters will be: (i) 9⅞in (250mm); (ii) 6¹/₁₆in (154mm); (iii) 3¹³/₁₆in (96mm); (iv) 2⁵/₁₆in (58mm); (v) 1½in (38mm); (vi) ¾in (20mm). **Please note that the imperial conversions are not precise. If you prefer to work in inches, an accurate imperial measured drawing is recommended.** As these parts are hand-turned some fitting of the joined pieces will be necessary to bring the parts to a consistent whole.

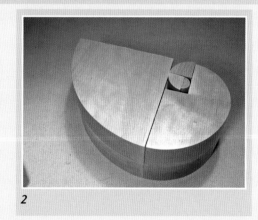

2

3 The production of the first three parts is exactly the same, only the diameters differ, therefore I will detail the method for the turning the first part and provide brief instruction for the next three. The same applies for the remaining three parts.

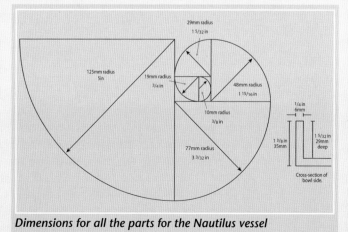

Dimensions for all the parts for the Nautilus vessel

Preparation

Part i

From hardwood which has been planed on its side and edge cut two pieces each 10³/₄in (270mm) long by 5³/₈in (135mm) wide by 1⁹/₁₆in (40mm) thick. Glue these blanks together, along their planed edges, with a newspaper/glue joint so that a 10³/₄in (270mm) square blank is produced. Allow the glue to dry.

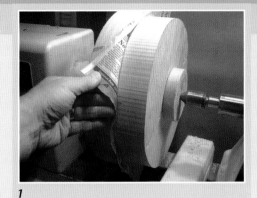

1

1 On that blank mark out and cut a 10³/₄in (270mm) circle, making sure that the compass point is located on the newspaper/glue joint line. Fit a 12in (300mm) diameter, 2in (50mm) thick softwood disc to a faceplate. Fix the prepared hardwood blank to the softwood faceplate using the newspaper/glue method. Make sure that the marked centre of the hardwood blank is held exactly on centre.

The picture shows the piece glued in place with a block used to spread the pressure on the centred blank. Leave until the glue is dry. Turn the hardwood disc round. Turn the face of the blank fully flat.

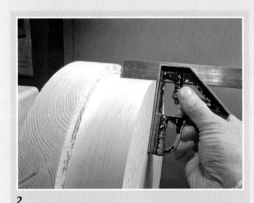

2

2 Turn the blank down to 9⁷/₈in (250mm) diameter, making sure that the edge is square to the face.

3

3 On the face of the work mark a pencil line ¹/₄in (6mm) in from the edge. Using a square-end tool, turn on the inside of the marked line to a starting depth of ¹³/₁₆in (20mm).

4 Turn out the inside of the hollow using a gouge. Square up the edge using the square-end tool until a flat-bottomed 1⁵/₃₂in (29mm) deep recess is turned. The picture shows the depth being measured. Sand and polish the inside and side (but not the top edge). On the polished side mark a pencil line 1³/₈in (35mm) measured from the top edge.

4

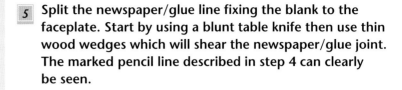

5

5 Split the newspaper/glue line fixing the blank to the faceplate. Start by using a blunt table knife then use thin wood wedges which will shear the newspaper/glue joint. The marked pencil line described in step 4 can clearly be seen.

6

6 Clean off the face of the softwood disc and mark a 9$\frac{7}{8}$in (250mm) diameter pencil circle on its face. On the inside of that pencil circle, using a square-end tool, turn a $\frac{1}{4}$in (6mm) wide groove $\frac{13}{16}$in (20mm) deep.

7

7 Fit the edge of the turned blank into this turned groove and adjust if necessary so that the blank will fit and can be firmly held in this jam chuck.

Apply small tacks of hot-melt glue between the softwood and hardwood discs to give extra grip.

8

8 Turn the hardwood face down to the marked 1$\frac{3}{8}$in (35mm) pencil line, making sure that the face is flat and true. Sand and polish the face.

9

9 To remove the finished disc pick off the hot-melt glue tacks. The polished surface should allow the glue tacks to peel away easily. If there is a problem with removing those glue tacks, unscrew the softwood faceplate, with the disc attached, take it to a microwave and heat on full power for 20 seconds. This should soften the glue enough for easy removal.

10

10 Split the newspaper/glue joint to produce two identical halves.

Part ii

1. Prepare the blank from two pieces of hardwood 6³/₈in (160mm) long by 3³/₁₆in (80mm) wide by 1⁹/₁₆in (40mm) thick. Glue the edges together with a newspaper/glue joint to make a blank 6³/₈in (160mm) square and leave to dry. When dry, cut a 6³/₈in (160mm) disc and glue that disc (newspaper/glue joint) to a wood faceplate. Make sure that the glue line is exactly on centre.

2. Turn the face flat and true, and reduce the whole to an exact 6¹/₁₆in (154mm) diameter making sure that the edge is square to the face. Sand and polish the edge. Measure, and mark a pencil line, ¹/₄in (6mm) in from the edge. On the inside of that line, using a square-end tool, turn in to a starting depth of ³/₈in (9mm).

3. Using a gouge turn out, on the inside of this groove, to a depth of 1⁵/₃₂in (29mm). Sand and polish the interior but not the top edge.

4. From the top edge measure 1³/₈in (35mm) down and mark in pencil around the edge. Carefully split the newspaper/glue joint to remove the piece.

5. Turn the face of the softwood disc flat and true. Into that face turn a 6¹/₁₆in (154mm) diameter groove, ¹/₄in (6mm) wide, ¹³/₁₆in (20mm) deep. Test and fit the turned blank into that groove using tacks of hot-melt glue to secure the piece. Turn the face of the blank, flat and true, down to the pencil line then sand and polish.

6. Pick off the hot-melt glue tacks and remove the finished piece.

7. The newspaper/glue joint may now be split.

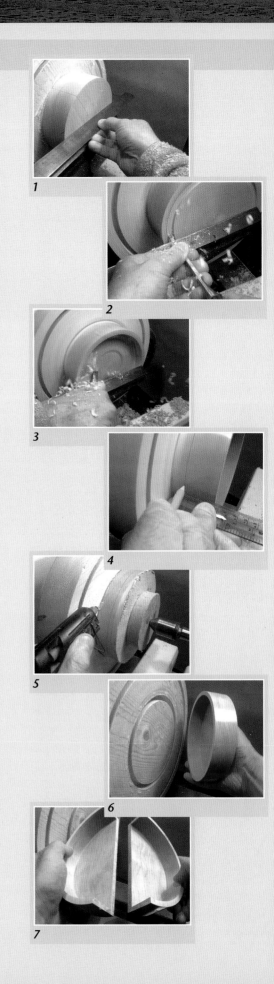

Part iii

Part (iii) is turned the same way. The blank is glued up (newspaper/glue joint) from two pieces each 4in (100mm) long by 2in (50mm) wide by 1^{9}/$_{16}$in (40mm) thick. The dimensions of the finished piece are: diameter 3^{13}/$_{16}$in (96mm), thickness 1^{3}/$_{8}$in (35mm), internal hollow 1^{5}/$_{32}$in (29mm) deep by 3^{5}/$_{16}$in (84mm) internal diameter. Using a newspaper/glue joint, fix the blank centrally onto the softwood faceplate, then proceed as before.

Parts iv – vi

Turning parts (iv), (v) and (vi) follows the same pattern as before except that they are not hollowed. The blank sizes for each are as follows:

For part (iv), two pieces 2^{3}/$_{4}$in (70mm) long by 1^{3}/$_{8}$in (35mm) wide by 1^{9}/$_{16}$in (40mm) thick. Newspaper/glue joined edge to edge producing a 2^{3}/$_{4}$in (70mm) square blank.

For part (v), two pieces 2in (50mm) long by 1in (25mm) wide by 1^{9}/$_{16}$in (40mm) thick. Newspaper/glue joined edge to edge producing a 2in (50mm) square blank.

For part (vi), two pieces 1^{7}/$_{32}$in (30mm) long by ^{19}/$_{32}$in (15mm) wide by 1^{9}/$_{16}$in (40mm) thick. Newspaper/glue joined edge to edge producing a 1^{7}/$_{32}$in (30mm) square blank.

1

The accurate turned diameter for (iv) is 2^{5}/$_{16}$in (58mm), for (v) is 1^{1}/$_{2}$in (38mm) and (vi) is ^{13}/$_{16}$in (20mm).

The pieces are each in turn centrally fixed to the softwood faceplate using a newspaper/glue joint then turned and split from the faceplate and set aside. The softwood faceplate can then be used as a jam chuck but the smallest diameter piece (vi) is turned to thickness first.

2

The jam-fit hollow is then widened to accept the intermediate sized piece (v) so it can be turned to thickness followed by piece (iv). The picture shows part (v) held in the jam chuck with hot-melt tacks being applied.

3 Here part (v) is turned to 1³⁄₈in (35mm) thick.

3

4 This shows the finished part (v) removed from the jam chuck.

4

5 The jam-chuck hole is now opened to accept part (iv), which will be tacked in place using hot-melt glue.

5

6 The end face is turned, bringing the thickness to 1³⁄₈in (35mm).

6

7 The glue tacks can be rubbed from the surface. The turned parts are then split.

7

8 The parts shown here are sufficient to make one Nautilus vessel, but of course you have made enough for two.

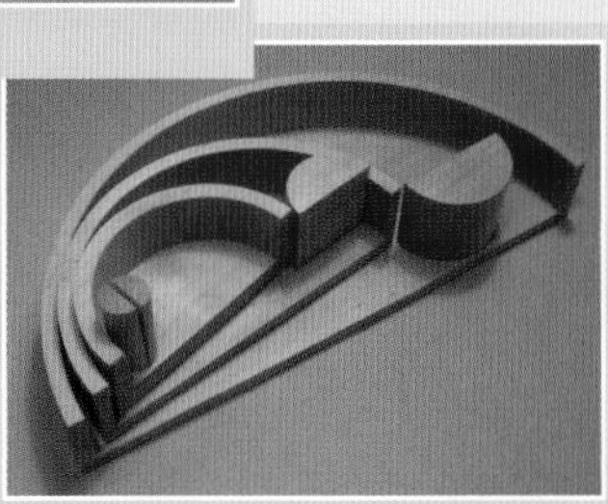

8

Fitting the parts together

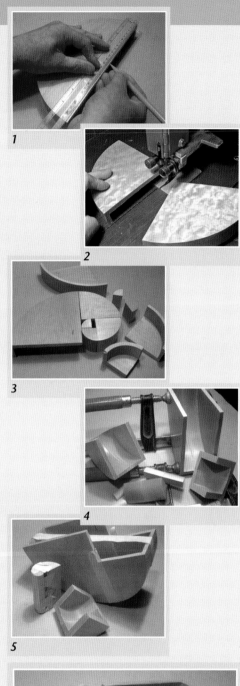

1 Having split the parts in half along the newspaper/glue joint, they now need to be cut again to produce quarters. Measure along the split centre line and mark the exact centre. Place a try square with its stock against the split edge and the straight edge in line with the marked centre line. Mark a pencil line at 90° to that edge.

2 Take each piece to the bandsaw and carefully cut along the marked pencil line. Here you can see a beautiful piece of quilted maple being cut.

3 As a quick try-out, assemble the parts dry. Adjustments can be made to any parts which do not quite fit.

4 Before these quarters are glued together to produce the Nautilus, the sawn and split edges need to be carefully sanded flat. The quarters may now be glued and clamped together using white carpenter's glue.

5 As the parts to be glued together will be endgrain edge to endgrain edge, I use a polyurethane glue for strength. Masking tape is used to hold the parts together whilst the glue sets. They are assembled in small sections which are allowed to dry.

6 The now dried sections can then be fitted together. Once the glue has fully set the piece may be sanded flat and repolished. Two Nautilus vessels are produced from this process, so the effort made and time spent are well rewarded with a pair of most unusual pieces from the lathe.

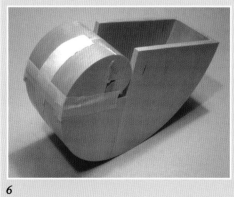

Prof. Johannes Volmer – Elliptical Conicon

Bob Rollings – Sphericon with Inlay

Bob Rollings – Hexagonal Tunbridge Stickware Sphericon

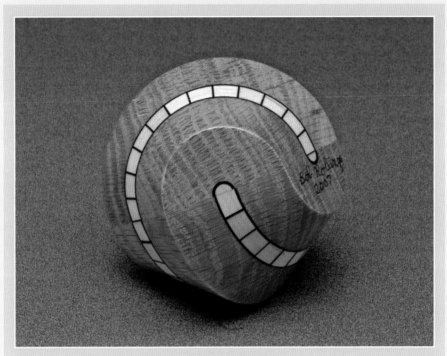

Bob Rollings – Hexagonal Streptohedron with Inlay

Bob Rollings – Four-Star Hybrid Streptohedron Earrings

Bob Rollings – Four-Point Streptohedron

Bob Rollings – Six-Arm Streptohedron with Inlaid Spots

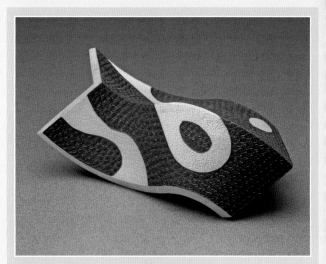

Pablo Nemzoff – Decorated Wave Bowl

David Springett – Snowflake Cross-Section Streptohedron using prototype engineering technique

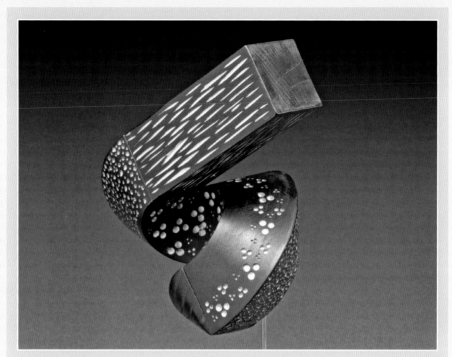

Ambrose and Brid O'Halloran – Decorated Knot Streptohedron

Malcolm Tibbetts – Tolerance.
Visit his website at: www.tahoeturner.com/gallery/52.html

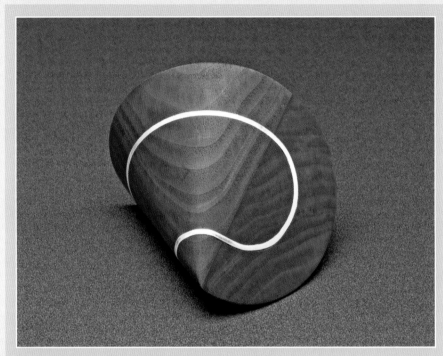

Bob Rollings – Conicon with Inlaid Aluminium Line

Bob Rollings – Sphericon with Inlaid Dots

Bob Rollings – Laminated Pentagonal Streptohedron

ob Rollings – Three-Point Streptohedron

Bob Rollings – Four-Point Hybrid Streptohedron

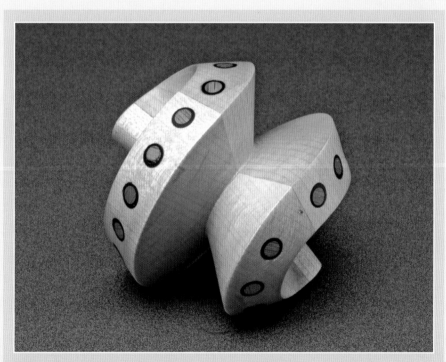

Bob Rollings – Five-Arm Streptohedron with Inlaid Dots

About the Author

A former woodwork teacher, David Springett has been a professional woodturner for more than 25 years. Specializing at first in lace bobbins, he became increasingly attracted to more experimental work, such as the seemingly impossible pieces described in his first book *Woodturning Wizardry*. He has demonstrated his woodturning techniques throughout the UK and USA, Canada, Germany, Israel and Ireland. In 2005 he was asked to present a paper, detailing his work on streptohedrons, to the Bridges Maths Symposium in London. In 2007 he was invited to exhibit some of his turned sculptural pieces at Intersculpt 2007 at the Ecole Nationale Supérieure des Arts et Métiers in Paris. This is David's fifth woodturning book.

david@cdspringett.fsnet.co.uk

Acknowledgements

I would like to acknowledge the help given to me by the following friends: Dan Crowe, John Davenport, Jean Francois Escoulen, Colin Hovland, James McMenemey, Pablo Nemzoff, Ambrose and Brid O'Halloran, Stephen Haynes, Howard Overton, Graeme Priddle, Peter Rand, Colin Roberts, Bob Rollings, John Sharp, Simon Smallwood, Jonathan Smith, Robin Springett, Bill Thurlow, Malcolm Tibbetts, Professor Johannes Volmer, Ross Weir and my wife Christine Springett. I would particularly like to thank Colin Roberts for his original thought.

Credits: *Pictured on page 2 are works by the following turners: Pablo Nemzoff, Brid and Ambrose O'Halloran, Bob Rollings, Prof. Johannes Volmer and David Springett. Elliptically turned ribbon forms on page 12 by Prof. Johannes Volmer. Elliptically turned conicon on page 16 by Prof. Johannes Volmer and decorated conicon and sphericon by Bob Rollings. Decorated streptohedrons on page 24 by Bob Rollings.*

Index

Names of illustrated pieces of work have been printed in *italics*.

GMC Publications

Castle Place, 166 High Street, Lewes, East Sussex BN7 1XU United Kingdom

Tel: +44 (0)1273 488005

Website: www.gmcbooks.com